answerable style

~~~~~~

~~~~~~~~~~~~~~~~~~~~~~~~~~ ❦ ARNOLD STEIN

~~~~~~

answerable style

~~~~~~

❦ Essays on PARADISE LOST

~~~~~~

~~~~~~

The University of Minnesota Press ❦
Minneapolis

Library of Congress Catalog Card Number: 53-5944

To Robert Penn Warren

PREFACE

I HAVE heard a professor of anatomy — I am told he is an excellent one — make the shocking statement that few surgeons "know" anatomy. I have no doubt that he is right, by his standards of anatomical knowledge, and it would not comfort me in engaging a surgeon to speculate on what he does not know about anatomy. But I should think he had better be engaged to practice his craft with the limited anatomy he knows, if he knows surgery and has some living recommendations; and engaged perhaps in his present state of competence, before some other specialists worry me out of the possibility of decision by reminding me that this surgeon does not really know their important specialties.

I have heard a distinguished Miltonist, whose distinction I recognize and respect, urge the claim of "all those studies of Milton's life and thought, and of his religious and intellectual background . . . to be heard before we pass final judgment on the poet — before, indeed, we can pretend fully to understand any one of his poems." My answer, which I certainly do not intend to be disrespectful of knowledge, is this: If we wait until we fully "understand" any major poem, when shall we be ready? The world created by a work of art requires contemplation from us, but it also requires action in the form of critical statement. We must always "pretend" to imaginative understanding, for it is only through the actual effort that our imagination may be engaged. Nor does "pretending" exclude consciousness of what we are doing. I should like to go further and say that I believe the critic's task of exploring the imaginative meaning is like the artist's task of submitting his ideas and vision to the order of words and form. Both must "pretend fully to understand" even while they are engaged in the process of imaginative understanding.

What Milton created, in spite of his immense debts to his cultural past, was no mere historical act but an act of the imagination that made the past present, and future. In our efforts to understand that act — which had better *not* exclude an effort to understand Milton's past — we must remember that we, like Milton, also have our roots in time. At the very best, *we* begin with a twentieth-century imagination, and we cannot make our present past if we cannot make the past present. The critical task is perhaps more like the poet's, to make the past present. I have not tried to be a seventeenth-century reader of *Paradise Lost*. I have tried to accept my role as a twentieth-century reader who is a student of seventeenth-century literature — one who finds himself at home with modern literature and modern criticism, at home but not therefore passively uncritical. I have honestly tried to enter Milton's mind and to submit myself to his work, but I have thought I could do so best if I did not surrender (or attempt to deceive myself that I had) the disciplines and sensibility I have gained from other poets: from Shakespeare, from Donne, Herbert, and Marvell, from Yeats and Eliot, to mention some of my major instructors. I think I have not remade Milton in any of their images. I think I have not denied the right of the seventeenth century to criticize the twentieth century. It is for the reader to judge. He will find that in my essay on Milton's style I have been instructed by Milton to challenge some widely held critical opinions — including some I have held.

I offer these statements to explain in part the position from which I begin. I do not intend, I hope I have not tried in the course of the book to persuade the reader of the merits of my approach. My purpose has been a critical interpretation of *Paradise Lost*, not a demonstration of my approach. I ask the reader to accept my point of view — which means chiefly, I think, my choice of the critical problems and how to approach them — not for itself but for its usefulness in interpreting *Paradise Lost*.

Perhaps I should say something about the order of these essays. This is the order in which they were conceived and written. It was mostly a matter of seeing problems and attempting solutions — with my solutions at their best providing me with the perspective to recognize more important problems and the means of possibly solving them. For instance, the first three essays deal chiefly with Satan and the problem of evil. From these I learned, among other things, how to see the problems of Paradise and the Fall. My final essay, on the style, is the least limited in scope: partly because it is the most ambitious, and partly because it has the advantage of everything learned from the preceding studies. For instance, in that essay some of my observations on Satan go beyond what I was able to say earlier. I might mention that I have not included the first two essays I wrote on *Paradise Lost*. The first (published in *ELH*, 1949) I now regard as having been useful mostly to me, as part of my workshop. The second, a study of the style, I later recognized as premature and withdrew from publication in the *Kenyon Review*. Three of the present essays, in slightly different form, have already been published. For permission to reprint them I am grateful to the editors of *PMLA*, *ELH*, and the *Kenyon Review*.

My debts are by now hard to trace — to students who asked questions or looked unconvinced; to scholars and critics I have agreed and disagreed with; to those who helped me avoid errors I should otherwise have made; to Miss Rosemond Tuve and Mr. A. S. P. Woodhouse for some forthright criticism (indirectly delivered, by Mr. W. R. Parker) from which I was able to profit; to Mr. Brents Stirling, who read some of the essays in manuscript; to my teacher and friend, Mr. Douglas Bush, even if he had not read the manuscript; to Mr. John Crowe Ransom, for encouragement and for lessons in critical deportment.

April 1953　　　　　　　　　　　　　　　　　　A. S.
Seattle, Washington

CONTENTS

answerable style

SATAN

C.S. Lewis & Chas. Williams   Tillyard

ONE need not choose between Satan's being a tragic hero or an absurd villain. Either extreme stamps us as a more restricted moralist than Milton the poet. For then we are less able than Milton to admit the test of contradiction into the moral universe of our art. If Satan is a tragic hero, it is because we are not honestly willing to test good by evil. If Satan is merely an absurd villain, it is because we want to ground our art upon too narrow a certainty; it is because we prefer the idea, and the confirmation of our certainty, to the more comprehensive, and therefore more daring, exploration of human experience — the submitting of an idea to a dramatic structure. If Satan is merely absurd, then we are not willing, though Milton is, to test evil by good.

The good in Satan responds to, and struggles toward, the good he encounters outside him. His evil is not pure; it can win the struggle against good only by allying itself with good. The rebellion which leads to the fall is in the _name of_ liberty, and against the _name_ of tyranny. His remorse, pity, tears all pay homage to good, but are perverted. If we do not give Satan his due, we cannot understand the nature of his evil. As Milton expresses it in *Areopagitica*: "look how much we thus expell of sin, so much we expel of virtue: for the matter of them both is the same; remove that, and ye remove them both alike." Even after we have recognized the inadequacy of Satan's tears, we must admit that they provide us with an impressive example of tears such as angels

but not so

3

weep. And though Satan's courage before Death must be recognized as a limited virtue, still we should not deny ourselves the pleasure of admiring his courage, nor deny ourselves the tension of seeing a virtue that is magnificent but futile once higher values have been rejected. It is true that Satan is already damned, that he has already felt (and as soon despised) pain; but still his courage is a fact. If we allow ourselves to admire his physical courage we shall have a better idea of what is wrong with his moral courage.

Should we apply strict logic to Satan, as though he were a philosophical position instead of a dramatic character, then of course he could not escape absurdity. Under those circumstances the most he, or any character, might hope for would be logical consistency.

> So farwel Hope, and with Hope farwel Fear,
> Farwel Remorse: all Good to me is lost;
> Evil be thou my Good.   (IV, 108ff)

This is absurd, as C. S. Lewis demonstrates with perhaps more vigor than necessary. But the absurd is not a simple absolute. Above all, it is not static. There is a difference between Dogberry's "write me down an ass" and Falstaff's "they hate us youth." The degree of self-consciousness, and the total situation, determine the quality and the effect of the absurd. Compare, for instance, Lady Macbeth's ignorant "Stop up th' access and passage to remorse" with Macbeth's partly self-conscious absurdities: "But wherefore could not I pronounce 'Amen'?" or "What hands are here?" or "Wake Duncan with thy knocking! I would thou couldst!" Satan, one may well feel, is partly aware of his absurdity, but he is unaware of the total situation, and he cannot master it by means of glib irony. Yet to dismiss him as ridiculous is also to dismiss him as a dramatic character, without allowing ourselves to experience his failure. That is to substitute logical judgment for dramatic experience.

Let us follow the development of one of Satan's failures. His role as leader seems to be a chief dramatic means of expressing his pride. "Faithful to whom?" is Gabriel's taunt after Satan is

discovered at Eve's ear practicing his responsibilities as leader.
The faith that goes only downward, never upward, exacts its
penalties; and Satan is tied to his followers more than he realizes.
In his most honest facing of self, at the beginning of Book IV,
he goes beyond the trap of his responsibility downward. He cannot repent, he says, because of his "dread of shame" before his
followers. That is a real enough barrier for Satan, but he pene-
trates beyond the active symbol of his pride to the basic mystery
of his pride itself. If God should grant him grace, he would only
fall again, more heavily. And so he touches the root of his despair,
and sees through to the unchanging quality of his fatal flaw. But
Satan's vision of himself is not steady. When he pulls back from
the desperate realization of what his pride means, it is only to
clutch harder the illusions of his responsibility. In the soliloquy
that soon follows, after Satan has been touched by the beauty of
Adam and Eve, it is "public reason," his duty as leader, that justifies his decision:

> And should I at your harmless innocence
> Melt, as I doe, yet public reason just,
> Honour and Empire with revenge enlarg'd,
> By conquering this new World, compels me now
> To do what else though damnd I should abhorre.   (IV, 388ff)

The tears and remorse that Satan was able to convert to oratory
return to plague him once he is separated from his audience of
followers. There seems reason for believing that the main difference between the Satan of the first two books and the later Satan
is the difference between a leader making a public appearance and
a leader on a solitary mission. That Satan is less magnificent away
from his followers hardly proves a falling-off in Milton's creative
powers, or a sudden realization that his villain has been getting
the best lines. The paradox is true to life: the leader has greater
stature when he is before his millions, but partly through being
forced to deny his essential solitary self (even while taking self
as the standard of measure). When Satan speaks in soliloquy it is
the solitary self speaking, still capable of despair and pity; but
the relationship holds: the pride that will not submit to superior

forces outside itself ends by submitting to inferior forces, also outside itself. It maintains the illusion of pure selfishness by being the will upon which others are dependent, but it cannot escape depending upon their dependence.

And so the evil of selfish pride is tested by the good of selfless devotion. The irony of that situation resides in the necessity of the test; it is also in the dramatic result of the test. But let us see what happens. After the leader's heroic public appearances, and the solitary heroism of his expedition through chaos, some of the first impetus begins to waver, and the solitary unheroic self can bring the conflict to articulation. The despair turns into desperate resolution; true repentance is impossible for him and so he must persevere in the course of action. Still, a little later the unsubdued good in him responds to the beauty of Adam and Eve; but evil has allies: pity can slide into self-pity, individual responsibility can be shifted to God, and the best argument of all, selfless dedication to the public cause, can marshal him the way he was going.

This argument helps keep alive the symbolic relationship between leader and followers. Again in Book IX, after he has returned, "cautious of day," from pacing the dark hemisphere for the sabbath which precedes his work, he falls into another fit of despair at the beauty of man's earth. But he comes to terms with his destiny and thinks once more as a leader, though this time he emphasizes the fruits of responsibility:

> To mee shall be the glorie sole among
> The infernal Powers, in one day to have marr'd
> What he *Almightie* styl'd, six Nights and Days
> Continu'd making, and who knows how long
> Before had bin contriving. (IX, 135ff)

A little while later, after he has been rendered "stupidly good" by Eve's beauty, he shifts his pronoun to the plural as a significant self-reminder of his duty:

> Thoughts, whither have ye led me, with what sweet
> Compulsion thus transported to forget
> What hither brought us. (IX, 473ff)

6

But Satan's pious concern for the responsibility of leadership is, as we have already seen, a complicated attitude, and one he is, perforce, dependent upon. It is a kind of talisman that he must protect, even at the cost of speaking truth. To defend the inviolability of his leadership he will reveal a state secret. When Gabriel taunts him with having abandoned his legions, Satan promptly drops his lie and reveals his mission of seeking a better abode for his followers. The language of defensive pride is significant. It behooves, he says,

> A faithful Leader, not to hazard all
> Through wayes of danger by himself untri'd.
> I therefore, I alone first undertook
> To wing the desolate Abyss.   (IV, 933ff)

From the beginning Satan displays a marked inclination to shift responsibility. It is all God's fault, he says in his first long public speech:

> but still his strength conceal'd,
> Which tempted our attempt, and wrought our fall.   (I, 641f)

This of course is public speech, a fulfillment of his accepted public responsibility; but it serves, we feel, to raise the speaker's own "fainting courage." As a leader, before his followers, Satan shifts the responsibility to God. And alone, Satan will blame God for Satan's vengeance on Adam, and for Paradise's being inadequately fenced. And alone, Satan will use the responsibility of his office as leader to shift the responsibility to his followers, to "public reason." He is dodging his own shadow, on a merry-go-round.

According to Milton's conception of evil, Satan's fate should evolve in two ways: the good he brings to others and the harm he brings to himself. Some passages from the *Christian Doctrine* provide the best commentary:

Nor does God make that will evil which was before good, but the will being already in a state of perversion, he influences it in such a manner, that out of its own wickedness it either operates good for others, or punishment for itself, though unknowingly, and with the intent of producing a very different result.   (Chapter VII)

Guiltiness, accordingly, is accompanied or followed by terrors of conscience . . . whence results a diminution of the majesty of the human countenance, and a conscious degradation of mind. (Chapter XIII)

This death [spiritual death] consists, first, in the loss . . . of that right reason . . . in which consisted as it were the life of the understanding. It consists, secondly, in that deprivation of righteousness and liberty to do good, and in that slavish subjection to sin and the devil, which constitutes, as it were, the death of the will. (Chapter XII)

Satan recognizes and rebels against the part of the moral law that may bring good out of evil. His statement, with its clear enunciation of the issue, comes early in Book I:

> To do ought good never will be our task,
> But ever to do ill our sole delight
> As being the contrary to his high will
> Whom we resist. If then his Providence
> Out of our evil seek to bring forth good,
> Our labour must be to pervert that end,
> And out of good still to find means of evil.   (I, 159ff)

The scope of the epic does not permit Satan ever to realize, dramatically, that good is brought about through his evil. He does envy the beauty of the world and guess that it is a compensation for his fall, but he does not experience, at least in *Paradise Lost,* the truth that Adam inherits blessings through Satan's crime against him. What Satan does experience, and dramatically, is the other part of the moral law, his own failure. The development of Satan's realization begins in Book I, with the evidences of inner conflict. It concludes in Book X with the short-lived triumph of Satan's return to hell — with the histrionic mounting of the throne incognito; with the distorted emphasis of his report, as if it were to his credit to have turned the trick with an absurd apple; with the final mass metamorphosis of all the devils into serpents.

Though Satan comes to realize much of his failure, part of his punishment is the self-punishment, "though unknowingly," of the moral (and dramatic) law. He is so highly self-conscious about some things that the petty lapses of his mind become significant betrayals that he is unaware of what is happening to him. "O indignitie!" he says at the thought that man has angels as his servants, but by the time Satan has rounded out his sentence the real source of the indignity is revealed:

> O indignitie!
> Subjected to his service Angel wings,
> And flaming Ministers to watch and tend
> Thir earthie Charge: Of these the vigilance
> I dread.   (IX, 154ff)

Satan contradicts himself; he was created by God and he wasn't. He is indignant at having to "imbrute" himself as a serpent, apparently forgetting that he has already had this experience before, without indignation. He is the victim (or patient) of his own eloquence, and it is not always magnificent eloquence. At one point he admits that only in destroying can he find "ease." But, in priming himself for the temptation of Eve, he talks as though destroying is more than a passive relief: it is called his only pleasure and joy.

Satan's reasoning, often shaky, suffers most from the kind of sustained naked exposure it receives in Book IX. There is no forensic necessity to cover this:

> O Earth, how like to Heav'n, if not preferr'd
> More justly, Seat worthier of Gods, as built
> With second thoughts, reforming what was old!
> For what God after better worse would build?   (IX, 99ff)

Satan, like Adam after he has decided to eat the apple, is reasoning from a special position – himself. He puts himself in God's place by putting God in Satan's place, and reasoning from there. The passage continues with more of the same:

> hee to be aveng'd
> And to repair his numbers thus impair'd,
> Whether such vertue spent of old now faild
> More Angels to Create, if they at least
> Are his Created or to spite us more,
> Determin'd to advance into our room

9

    A Creature form'd of Earth, and him endow,
    Exalted from so base original,
    With Heav'nly spoils, our spoils.   (IX, 143ff)

It is a masterly presentation of Satan's psychology, in Satan's terms. And he — "unknowingly" — accepts his own trivial reasoning, or the part that suits his needs; for a few lines further on he states, without reservation or alternative, that man was created to spite the fallen angels. It is like Iago's accepting what he has previously advanced as a tentative possibility.

These examples lead us to the major exhibition of what happens to Satan's mind. We remember his trumpeting challenge, "A mind not to be chang'd by Place or Time." And we see what he cannot see, that he is diminished in mind, and in that important sense changed. But the irony does not stop there, for Satan's mind is both changed and unchanged.

    The mind is its own place, and in it self
    Can make a Heav'n of Hell, a Hell of Heav'n.   (I, 254f)

He is only partly right, but he also speaks truer than he knows. The not-to-be-changed part of his mind cannot prevent him from feeling a kind of terror at the sight of Eve's beauty, and he acknowledges that there is terror in both love and beauty. We understand Satan's fear, and the irony of his situation, when we remember Raphael's lecture on love. Through love, he told Adam, we refine the thoughts, enlarge the heart; love has its seat in the reason, and is the ladder by which we ascend to heavenly love. No wonder Satan backs away, and has to arm himself with hate — to protect the "unchangeable" part of his mind in its program for taking over. What Satan intended as a declaration of mental freedom turns out to be freedom only to pursue the blind impetus of evil action. The true liberty of inward freedom (which is always "twinned" with right reason) is lost to him: the trap of leadership and the compulsions of the moral law impose upon him the restricted course of action that constitutes the loss of his outward freedom. It is the "death of the will." Satan is ironically deceived by his ability to move, and still powerfully; but the power is that of a concentrated impetus, along a narrow chute, unable to control its rushing speed toward its own destruction.

"*A mind not to be chang'd by Place or Time*": "*The mind is its own place.*" Both Belial and Mammon end their long speeches opposing continued war against heaven with the same argument, presumably their best: adjust to the environment.

> or enur'd not feel,
> Or chang'd at length, and to the place conformd
> In temper and in nature, will receive
> Familiar the fierce heat, and void of pain;
> This horror will grow milde, this darkness light.   (II, 216ff)

> Our torments also may in length of time
> Become our Elements, these piercing Fires
> As soft as now severe, our temper chang'd
> Into their temper; which must needs remove
> The sensible of pain.   (II, 274ff)

It is not an argument that Satan can afford to consider. But it is the position to which he is, unknowingly, reduced when he is tortured by the beauty of the earth:

> the more I see
> Pleasures about me, so much more I feel
> Torment within me, as from the hateful siege
> Of contraries; all good to me becomes
> Bane, and in Heav'n much worse would be my state.
>
> (IX, 119ff)

This development could not emerge in hell proper; besides, there his position required a bold, complete front. But the circle has now closed; he has adjusted so entirely to the "unchanged" part of his mind, the hell within, that he *needs* hell.

By way of conclusion let us leave structural analysis and turn to the style, where we can see in a couple of examples much of the idea of Satan's failure; for Milton's style is both the medium for dramatic structure and dramatic structure itself. After his soul-searching soliloquy at the beginning of Book IV, Satan proceeds toward the border of Eden. The verse leaves him for a long description of the beauties of that place, and then returns to find him apparently still shaken from the violence of his inner conflict.

> Now to th' ascent of that steep savage Hill
> *Satan* had journied on, pensive and slow. (IV, 172f)

The desperate resolution that ended the soliloquy did not, it would seem, end the conflict. There is no path through the under-growth, and only one gate on the other side:

> which when th' arch-fellon saw
> Due entrance he disdaind, and in contempt,
> At one slight bound high overleap'd all bound
> Of Hill or highest Wall, and sheer within
> Lights on his feet. As when a prowling Wolfe,
> Whom hunger drives to seek new haunt for prey,
> Watching where Shepherds pen thir Flocks at eeve
> In hurdl'd Cotes amid the field secure,
> Leaps o're the fence with ease into the Fould:
> Or as a Thief bent to unhoord the cash
> Of some rich Burgher, whose substantial dores,
> Cross-barrd and bolted fast, fear no assault,
> In at the window climbes, or o're the tiles;
> So clomb this first grand Thief into Gods Fould:
> So since into his Church lewd Hirelings climbe. (IV, 179ff)

Calling Satan the arch-felon seems like external commentary, or perhaps only a kind of decorative epithet. But it turns out to be an anticipation of the imagery. So too is the animal grace of the rhythm that carries Satan over the barrier to light on his feet. Then we are into the unfolding imagery. From contempt and ease to hunger and ease, to the vague itch of "bent to unhoord" and mere skulking trickery: Satan diminishes in the images. We have three views of him, each one breaking down the mask of his "contempt" and getting further into his inner nature — projecting (with the help of the "pensive and slow") Satan's own real self. It is a kind of counterpoint, the diminishing of Satan played against the increasing magnitude of the theft. It becomes the primal theft, in God's house, preparing the way for all subsequent theft.

Satan's drama continues, though again he disappears from the

verse while the garden and Adam and Eve are described. There
is one mention, a hundred lines further on, of his feelings — the
brief "Saw undelighted all delight." And then, about seventy
lines later, we return to him, still shaken:

> When *Satan* still in gaze, as first he stood,
> Scarce thus at length faild speech recoverd sad. (IV, 356f)

The impetus of the imagery is still working when Satan returns
to Eden in Book IX — the ease not lost, but the contempt gone:

> In with the River sunk, and with it rose
> Satan involv'd in rising Mist, then sought
> Where to lie hid. (IX, 74ff)

Or consider the following passage. The leader has just by the
power of his words recalled his fallen legions from the burning
flood:

> All these and more came flocking; but with looks
> Down cast and damp, yet such wherein appear'd
> Obscure som glimps of joy, to have found thir chief
> Not in despair, to have found themselves not lost
> In loss it self; which on his count'nance cast
> Like doubtful hue: but he his wonted pride
> Soon recollecting, with high words, that bore
> Semblance of worth not substance, gently rais'd
> Thir fainting courage, and dispel'd their fears. (I, 522ff)

If we fix our attention on what is said about the "high words," we
may not observe that Satan, in his role as leader, is being presented
dramatically. The key word is the repeated "cast." For Satan's
countenance reflects their looks, as his feelings reflect theirs. The
relationship between chief and followers is conveyed by the wonderful ambiguity of "Like doubtful hue." And the relationship
is extended by the next lines, which are an ironic demonstration
of the internal-external mutual relationship between looks and
feelings, theirs and Satan's. Satan cannot help himself. Leader-like
he subdues his own doubts, which he sees reflected in them (along
with their dependence upon him for hope). He *recollects*, with
an effort of will, his mainstay, the "wonted pride." (In Book IX,
after Satan has been forced, by the beauty and innocence of Eve,

to stand abstracted from his own evil, "stupidly good," he regains control of his will by recollecting himself: "Fierce hate he recollects.") He gently raises their (and by implication *his*) "fainting courage." The "high words" are like the pride, recollected by an effort of will. Is it an ignorant effort of will? Unless we are prepared to say so, then we must admit that Satan himself may be aware of the false worth of his words, and that the commentary may be internal, a projection of Satan's consciousness. Not that we must think Satan coolly rational about all this, for the irony lies in the trap of leadership: he may know better but he cannot act better, for he is caught in his own trap.

Satan's words are not given here, but we are not dependent on this passage alone for judging his degree of consciousness. After a military review plainly intended to bolster the morale of both troops and leader — the band plays in the Dorian mode, the warriors march "Breathing united force with fixed thought" — the focus returns to Satan. He takes heart from the sight of them, from their number: *his* strength. He towers and shines above them. But still, the tone of the passage changes, as do the details, when we move from the external public appearance of Satan as leader to his feelings as leader. The "dauntless" courage and "considerate" pride are there, but so are the scars, and the care, and the "faded cheek." The passage needs quoting:

> cruel his eye, but cast
> Signs of remorse and passion to behold
> The fellows of his crime, the followers rather
> (Far other once beheld in bliss) condemn'd
> For ever now to have their lot in pain,
> Millions of Spirits for his fault amerc't
> Of Heav'n, and from Eternal Splendors flung
> For his revolt, yet faithfull how they stood,
> Thir Glory witherd. . . .
> Thrice he assayd, and thrice in spite of scorn,
> Tears such as Angels weep, burst forth: at last
> Words interwove with sighs found out their way.   (I, 604ff)

This is a continuation of our previous insight into Satan's consciousness. In spite of the intervening eighty lines, with what they do to build up Satan's morale as leader, and to emphasize the external characteristics of his relations with his troops, the dramatic conflict within him has been continuing underneath all the surface show of the military review. The key word, "cast," is repeated. The ambiguity of Satan's earlier "Like doubtful hue" is resolved, and his feelings made explicit — remorse, passion, tears. His sense of responsibility as leader, indirectly conveyed in the earlier passage, becomes admitted guilt here; he even drops the mask of euphemism (as necessary in private as in public to the leader), and calls his fellows followers. The Latinate syntax, linking "behold" with "yet faithfull how they stood," perfectly suits the development of Satan's feelings. This must have been the main impulse of the remorse, but it can find out its way only after his confession of their status as followers, of their loss, of his guilt. The "high words," when he finally can speak them, are those of controlled and self-conscious eloquence, to soothe the emotions and build hope upon calm — by fine sounds and rhythms, by vague optimism, and by the specific assurance that the war will be continued "by fraud or guile" rather than by force. Satan knows that his words have only "Semblance of worth," but he speaks, through an effort of will, what is expected of the leader by his followers. He also speaks what is expected of the leader by the leader.

In the passages just considered the style has been dramatically functional in the fullest sense of that phrase. Only style could have been sensitive and flexible enough to communicate the complex conflict between Satan's internal feelings and the external necessities of his public position. The larger context is the hierarchy of absolute values. The conflict is between the private good within Satan (the remorse, passion, tears, guilt) and the public evil (his position as leader of the forces against good). But the evil is within him too, for his private position has determined his public one. And the private good, which refers to the larger context, also refers to the public evil, for Satan's remorse and guilt are chiefly directed toward his followers and his responsibility for their fall. So his private good is, in the hierarchy of values, a lesser good, for allegiance to his followers is less good than allegiance to God. The responsibility that Satan accepts is, in the scale of values, downward (to his followers) not upward (to God). And so the good which feels remorse and despair within, which struggles with the evil within and the evil without, finds its expression in a secondary good; but once the primary good is rejected, remorse becomes merely a sense of public responsibility, passion and tears become moving eloquence to carry out the public office of removing despair. Guilt gets lost in the shuffle.

THE WAR IN HEAVEN

IF THE war in heaven is approached as Milton's fulfillment of his epic obligations, if we regard it as a realistic war to be taken quite literally — then we cannot escape Dr. Johnson's verdict that the "confusion of spirit and matter" fills the whole narrative with "incongruity." How can we believe in the fiction of a raging battle in which immortal spirits uncomplainingly confine themselves in hindering armor and, in between verbal debates, use material weapons that lessen their might? But suppose the material action of the war does not exist for its literal and independent meaning, but is instead part of a complex metaphor? That is the view that this study proposes taking.

We are told before the narrative begins that it will be metaphorical:

> what surmounts the reach
> Of human sense, I shall delineate so,
> By lik'ning spiritual to corporal forms,
> As may express them best.   (V, 571ff)

But still, this is preceded by what seems to be an echo of Aeneas' polite prologue to Dido (which would anticipate a direct historical tale), and it is followed by Raphael's enigmatic questioning of the metaphor:

> though what if Earth
> Be but the shaddow of Heav'n, and things therein
> Each to other like, more then on earth is thought?
>
> (V, 574ff)

Presumably, though, the metaphor has not been discredited but further qualified, for when he concludes his account Raphael emphasizes the metaphorical point of view again: "Thus measuring things in Heav'n by things on Earth /At thy request." In between, besides the constant indirect touches more significant to fallen than to unfallen man, there have been some deliberate gestures toward the understanding of the immediate audience – some of them charming in their thoughtfulness (like grandfather translating remote events into the terms of grandchild's familiar experience). When God's legions march forth upon the air, it is as when all the birds came summoned "to receive / Thir names of thee." When heaven resounds, all the earth, "had Earth bin then," "had to her Center shook." When Michael and Satan meet, it is as if nature's concord should break and two opposing planets clash. But this, the deliberate framework of metaphor, does not take us far, though it invites us to build on the angel's hint.

From the opening of Book I the war in heaven seems more than a simple, finished event. In the invocation we have the authorized formal side presented: the war was ambitious, impious, proud, vain, and resulting in ruin. Satan's first speech implies that there was another side – even after we have partly discounted the personal tones of the defeated leader who speaks of the good old lost cause, "hazard in the Glorious Enterprize." That too is a formal side, presented by the losing actor in the drama. Then Satan goes on, to reveal, before he can pull himself together in defiance, something more:

> into what Pit thou seest
> From what highth fal'n, so much the stronger provd
> He with his Thunder: and till then who knew
> The force of those dire Arms?   (I, 91ff)

A little later the surprise has been bolstered with a kind of indignation:

> but still his strength conceal'd,
> Which tempted our attempt, and wrought our fall.   (I, 641f)

We soon learn that we cannot get answers in hell, but we begin to see certain questions, and the possibility that their answers may appear when we see the dramatic presentation of the rebellion. For one thing, Satan's "innumerable force" receives a definite tally later — it is only one third of the angels. And this fact will look different when we learn that God opposes the enemy force with an equal number only, and then puts a fixed limit on the individual strength of the contestants, and then sends only the Son against the rebels, and with His strength limited too. Satan puts so much store on his having shaken the throne of God, against "His utmost power" — "Who from the terrour of this Arm so late / Doubted his Empire" — that we begin to wait for the actual presentation of the conflict. In his long soliloquy at the beginning of Book IV, though Satan tells us much, he answers none of the questions he has raised in our minds about the war. His silence is no doubt a commentary; so complete a fact requires no mention, once the forensic necessity has been removed, but we cannot know this at the time.

The clash with Gabriel at the end of Book IV provides us with a sudden new viewpoint; it will prove to be a true anticipation of what happens in the battles, even though we cannot know this yet. For the first time, with Satan present, an actor on the scene, we see him entirely from the outside; and the external view is one of complete ridicule. It is Gabriel's

> O loss of one in Heav'n to judge of wise,
> Since *Satan* fell, whom follie overthrew. (IV, 904f)

The dominating spirit of the encounter, on both sides, is that of scornful ridicule. Gabriel's most telling point is directed at Satan's *discipline*. The fight itself never takes place because Satan, in spite of his blind defiance, has been forced by experience to recognize that ultimate *strength* is external. He obeys God's sign, even though he has just been defying, with words, God's chariot once more. Gabriel's final comment brings the three themes together again — strength, ridicule, discipline:

> *Satan*, I know thy strength, and thou knowst mine,
> Neither our own but giv'n; what follie then
> To boast what Arms can doe, since thine no more
> Then Heav'n permits, nor mine. (IV, 1006ff)

Perhaps this sounds like a piece of ceremonial tournament chivalry — at least to our merely human understanding. If so, it may be because the ceremony is made of symbolic gestures that are founded upon truth. It is not ceremony to Gabriel, but direct truth, the truth of innocent inexperience that has not (according to Satan's taunt) tried evil. And Satan has experienced that truth.

Within the larger frame of the angel's narration to Adam there is another major frame that governs our perspective of the rebellion. The dominant mood of the war is like nothing so much as a scherzo, a kind of great scherzo, like some of Beethoven's — with more than human laughter, too elevated, and comprehensive, and reverberating not to be terribly funny. God sets the mood when he comments to the Son on the budding rebellion:

> Neerly it now concernes us to be sure
> Of our Omnipotence, and with what Arms
> We mean to hold what anciently we claim
> Of Deitie or Empire . . .
> Let us advise, and to this hazard draw
> With speed what force is left, and all imploy
> In our defence, lest unawares we lose
> This our high place, our Sanctuarie, our Hill.   (V, 721ff)

The Son, as usual, reflects the Father's meaning:

> Mightie Father, thou thy foes
> Justly hast in derision, and secure
> Laugh'st at thir vain designes and tumults vain.   (V, 734ff)

Throughout the serious events of the foreground, in the spacious North, the great laugh, omniscient and uncircumscribed, cannot fail to be heard.

Before proceeding to the more central ridicule, and to some of the significant reverberations, it is worth noting how much of the war is conducted in terms of external ridicule. In one sense, at least, the conflict is between God's mockery and Satan's. Anticipations of this begin early. We have already noted the "till then who knew/ The force of those dire Arms" and the "tempted our attempt." There is the suggestive mockery (that is meant to do

more than perform its immediate practical function) when Satan
rouses his followers from the burning lake:

> or have ye chos'n this place
> After the toyl of Battel to repose
> Your wearied vertue, for the ease you find
> To slumber here, as in the Vales of Heav'n?
> Or in this abject posture have ye sworn
> To adore the Conquerour?   (I, 318ff)

We have testimony from the other fallen angels that ridicule
was an important attitude in the conflict. Moloch remembers

> When the fierce Foe hung on our brok'n Rear
> Insulting, and pursu'd.   (II, 78f)

(This is not literally accurate, but it has its truth; the "insulting"
I take to have both its familiar and its Latinate meaning. If Moloch
is mostly remembering what happened to him in a small skirmish,
when he fled bellowing (VI, 362), that makes an interesting, and
true, synecdoche.) To the extent that the conflict still exists,
ridicule continues to be an active attitude. Belial's precise verb,
in a context where any sort of resounding phrase might have been
expected, touches the situation metaphorically. God's legions
scout far and wide, he says, "Scorning surprize" (II, 134). And
God himself "All these our motions vain, sees and derides"
(II, 191). And Belial, for good measure, introduces his own God-
like imitated perspective of irony:

> I laugh, when those who at the Spear are bold
> And vent'rous, if that fail them, shrink and fear
> What yet they know must follow, to endure
> Exile, or ignominy, or bonds, or pain,
> The sentence of thir Conquerour.   (II, 204ff)

Still concerning ourselves with external ridicule, let us look at
the scenes in heaven for the beginnings of this attitude we have
been exploring. From the start it is not only God who mocks,
though God omnisciently sets the mood first. There are, of
course, the formal flytings traditional in literary battles, but these
do more than provide the usual variety and relief. They are part

of the complex structure of ridicule, the most external part of which consists in the frequent repetition of words denoting scorn, scoffing, laughter, deriding, contempt, disdain, vanity, and folly. The words reflect deeds, for besides the verbal abuse there is great laughter and counter-laughter in heaven. The laughter is symbolic action, but there is also real action that produces real laughter by the participants, besides the action that is intended to induce laughter in the reader.

If we think of the main events on their physical level alone (the other levels will make their significant comic additions), we shall see how consistent the line of ridicule is, and how close it approaches at times to what is almost a kind of epic farce. Satan's wound by the sword of Michael renders him physically ridiculous for the first time. His imbruting himself as a cormorant, as lion, as tiger; the more telling view of him, not *as* a toad, but without so much as the dignity of definition, merely the suggestive "Squat like a Toad"; the indirect view of his leaping into Paradise like a wolf or a thief — these views are less ridiculous through physical emphasis than they are through what is involved mentally and morally. (The fact that Satan later complains, as if for the first time, when he has to imbrute himself as a snake, helps bear this out.)

The wounding by Michael is parallel to Satan's first being exposed to complete ridicule by Gabriel, the Satan whom folly overthrew. Gabriel's ridicule is psychological, with physical overtones; Satan wounded is physically ridiculous, with psychological overtones (the difference between hitting any man, and a man proud of his bearing and composure, with a custard pie). The situation is physical, but we know Satan and his proclamation that the mind governs place — *is* place. Any physical discomfiture that he suffers will be most keenly felt in his mind. And though the material wound will heal without apparent scar, because of the vital nature of his "liquid texture," we are left to draw our own conclusions about the mental wound. We remember him "Gnashing for anguish and despite and shame." In physical terms alone this makes no sense, which is of course true of the whole war.

But the physical is part of the metaphorical view (the narrator's, to begin with) that always has nonphysical as well as physical meanings. Even when the climax of defeat is reached and the physical metaphor becomes reality, it is a reality that surpasses the physical through the agency of the physical. But that is to look too far ahead.

In one important scene (which we must later return to, on another level) the good angels are also exposed to physical ridicule, "Angel on Arch-Angel rowl'd" by the shot from Satan's cannon. The situation, with all its details, is quite unsparing:

> Foule dissipation follow'd and forc't rout;
> Nor serv'd it to relax thir serried files.
> What should they do? if on they rusht, repulse
> Repeated, and indecent overthrow
> Doubl'd, would render them yet more despis'd,
> And to thir foes a laughter; for in view
> Stood rankt of Seraphim another row
> In posture to displode thir second tire
> Of Thunder: back defeated to return
> They worse abhorr'd. *Satan* beheld thir plight,
> And to his Mates thus in derision call'd.   (VI, 598ff)

The physical ridicule is capped by verbal derision as Satan and Belial vie with each other at word-play. Then the physical comes back, in what at the moment seems to be the climax of the war, the battle of the landscape.

It is epic comedy, even on its physical level — elevated to the epic by magnificent imaginative power, made comic by controlled excess.

> From thir foundations loosning to and fro
> They pluckt the seated Hills with all thir load,
> Rocks, Waters, Woods, and by the shaggie tops
> Up lifting bore them in thir hands: Amaze,
> Be sure, and terrour seis'd the rebel Host,
> When coming towards them so dread they saw
> The bottom of the Mountains upward turn'd,
> Till on those cursed Engins triple-row
> They saw them whelmd, and all thir confidence
> Under the weight of Mountains buried deep,

> Themselves invaded next, and on thir heads
> Main Promontories flung, which in the Air
> Came shadowing. (VI, 643ff)

Part of the comic effect is in Milton's carefully interrupting the viewpoint at the crucial moment. We have the huge, comprehensive details of the rocks, waters, woods; and then the gigantic niceness of the detail that pictures the mountains, pulled up by the tops, coming bottom side up toward them (apparently in a slow arc, the way a shot is put). In between, we are forced to look away, to separate ourselves from the action, and see it as spectator, not as participator: "Amaze, / Be sure, and terrour . . ." (To introduce the custard pie again — we do not see it coming toward us and at the last moment hit the person behind us; instead, we are on the sideline watching the slow arc of the pie as it travels unerringly toward someone well off to our side; and then our eyes complete the arc before the pie does, so that we can watch the frozen amazement of the person who is the target as he watches the arc nearing completion.)

The scene reaches its height when the rebels reply in kind:

> So Hills amid the Air encountered Hills
> Hurl'd to and fro with jaculation dire,
> That under ground they fought in dismal shade;
> Infernal noise; Warr seem'd a civil Game
> To this uproar. (VI, 664ff)

Surely it is naive to think Milton straining for grandeur in this passage. That is to read this as if it were the sort of humorless exaggeration that Statius and Lucan can assault the reader with. The cumulative ridicule will not permit our doing so. Besides, the effect that Milton achieves is the effect of strain. Things have now been pushed to the utmost, beyond which all heaven might have "gone to wrack." If we do not regard this as humorless grandeur, we may suspect "jaculation" of being the kind of exaggerated word that is calculated to embarrass the exaggeration, after the manner more familiar in mock-epic. The fighting underground, which Milton may have picked up from Statius, and improved upon, is not presented as straight grandeur, but as both grand and grotesque. We cannot ignore the controlling effect of "infernal," here suddenly introduced to echo Satan's threat of making a hell of heaven, and to anticipate "Heav'n ruining from Heav'n." It is the approach to chaos, the result of the violence that heaven cannot brook, the strain to the point of cracking. But this is to move away from the physical level, which is our immediate concern. If we have been following the line of ridicule correctly so far, we are probably right in suspecting that the excess in this passage is laughing at an object: it is a materialistic concept of *might*. But to see what this means we must go on.

In the grand finale of physical ridicule the rebels are again left exposed to laughter by the interrupted point of view. The chariot of God rides over the "Shields and Helmes, and helmed heads" of the prostrate possessors,

> That wish'd the Mountains now might be again
> Thrown on them as a shelter from his ire.   (VI, 842f)

The Son checks His strength, not wishing to destroy but only to "root" them out of heaven. He raises up the overthrown (to heap new ridicule upon them):

> and as a Heard
> Of Goats or timerous flock together throngd
> Drove them before him Thunder-struck, pursu'd
> With terrors and with furies to the bounds
> And Chrystall wall of Heav'n, which op'ning wide,
> Rowld inward, and a spacious Gap disclos'd
> Into the wastful Deep; the monstrous sight
> Strook them with horror backward, but far worse
> Urg'd them behind; headlong themselves they threw
> Down from the verge of Heav'n, Eternal wrauth
> Burnt after them to the bottomless pit.   (VI, 856ff)

Never do they appear so ridiculous, not even as a timorous flock, as when they are caught isolated between the before and the behind.

The scene itself is magnificent and superhuman as an expression of wrath and physical force. But the violence that the rebels naively set in motion returns to deprive them of all superhuman grandeur, and then of merely human dignity (if man had been then). They descend, as in a series of explosions, the scale of creation. Though they have enough will to throw themselves down, as a herd of animals, they have been *rooted* out. It is "Heav'n ruining from Heav'n" — which seems to suggest the descent of spirit to matter, and of matter to the unformed matter of chaos, even to a kind of sub-chaos:

> confounded *Chaos* roard,
> And felt tenfold confusion in thir fall
> Through his wilde Anarchie, so huge a rout
> Incumberd him with ruin.   (VI, 871ff)

This is to be understood metaphorically, as the climax of their physical humiliation. It does not last, any more than their later mass metamorphosis into serpents, with which this is parallel. But it is a punishment, on the material level, for the material nature of their sin. If they regain their form in hell, that is because they regain free will (which has been interrupted by divine wrath). Spirits, we remember, "Cannot but by annihilating die." Incidentally, Bacon says the same thing about matter: "Annihilation and absolute Destruction cannot be effected but by the Omnipotency of God." Bacon's remarks on the cyclical behavior of matter may explain what is happening to the rebel angels. In their struggle to escape God's wrath they may be cooperating, or more, in the transformation. Matter, Bacon says (in commenting on the myth of Proteus, in *The Wisdom of the Ancients*), "being thus caught in the straits of Necessity, doth change and turn herself into divers strange Forms and Shapes of Things, so that at length (by fetching a Circuit as it were) she comes to a Period, and (if the Force continue) betakes herself to her former Being."

It is time to find a better term for what has been called *external* and *physical*. The ridicule on this level, as the last part of the discussion indicated, has its real (i.e., metaphorical) meaning in reference to the *material* — the lowest stage in the scale of matter, mind, and spirit. In spite of an arbitrary attempt to isolate the material level, it has been implicit, and sometimes explicit, that this level has its metaphorical meaning in reference to the other levels. As we proceed, the interrelationships will become more apparent and more complex. But first, with the perspective we have gained, let us look at the material level again.

"Our puissance is our own," Satan declares to Abdiel. It constitutes a denial of values outside the self and an assertion of the materialistic value of might. Raphael provides us with a choral commentary when he declines to name some of the rebel angels and their deeds, "In might though wondrous and in Acts of Warr":

> For strength from Truth divided and from Just,
> Illaudable, naught merits but dispraise
> And ignominie.   (VI, 381ff)

Might, elevated to an absolute, proves an impostor in the divine comedy once it comes face to face with the direct expression of God's will. The rebels must be taught in terms of the value they hold, and so they "learn, as likes them, to despise / God and *Messiah* his annointed King." The issue is formulated by the Son when he declares His reason for the solitary contest against the rebels:

> That they may have thir wish, to trie with mee
> In Battel which the stronger proves, they all,
> Or I alone against them, since by strength
> They measure all, of other excellence
> Not emulous, nor care who them excells.   (VI, 818ff)

As prelude to their materialistic punishment by the descent through chaos, the trampled rebels have their strength withered, their "wonted vigour" drained; they are left "Exhausted, spiritless."

But they sin against reason too, and so we may expect to find, on this second level, a pattern of ridicule running parallel to that on the materialistic level. It is still a conflict, however — Satan's ridicule of the mind matched against God's. As in hell, Satan is a great master of forensic irony. His opening speech for war, like the speech raising his followers from the burning lake, uses verbal

ridicule as if it were a lash—reversing, as it were, the nervous
process by making the mind tell the flesh that it hurts:

> Thrones, Dominations, Princedomes, Vertues, Powers,
> If these magnific Titles yet remain
> Not meerly titular, since by Decree
> Another now hath to himself ingross't
> All Power, and us eclipst under the name
> Of King anointed, for whom all this haste
> Of midnight march, and hurried meeting here,
> This onely to consult how we may best
> With what may be devis'd of honours new
> Receive him coming to receive from us
> Knee-tribute yet unpaid, prostration vile,
> Too much to one, but double how endur'd,
> To one and to his image now proclaim'd?   (V, 772ff)

Though we are most likely to think of Satan as a figure of pride
and unconquerable will, it is apparent that one of his views of
himself, a public view, is as a master of reason. And he can make
an appeal in the name of reason with no less assurance than in the
name of freedom. After the opening ridicule, intended to soften
up his audience by submitting them to what practically amounts
to physical pressure, he moves to the next stage, that of preparing them intellectually for the final stage, spiritual rebellion that
will complete the circle by expressing itself in physical rebellion.
It is significant that what Satan offers is an appeal to reason rather
than a demonstration, an appeal either in the form of loaded question or loaded statement:

> But what if better counsels might erect
> Our minds and teach us to cast off this Yoke?
> . . . .
>   ye will not, if I trust
> To know ye right, or if ye know your selves
> . . . .
>
> Who can in reason then or right assume
> Monarchie over such as live by right
> His equals, if in power and splendor less,
> In freedome equal?   (V, 785ff)

Pyrrhonian

But if Satan considers himself a master of reason, it seems to be
in a public way, for purposes of appeal, or debate, or ridicule. Actually, he seems to distinguish between the reason and what are to
him the higher functions of the mind. Reason is the most important means of destroying reason, and it is a major weapon of the
intellectual cynic. When Satan calls Abdiel "seditious Angel," he
is relishing his own humor; but he is also, shrewd relativist that
he is, undermining the possibility of judgment. Look, he is saying,
if I am a rebel, so are you; and if you look at it logically, one sin
is pretty much like another. Similarly, in the formal debate with
Abdiel, Satan, by way of introducing his heresy of self-generation,
accuses Abdiel of heresy. Satan's argument is an interesting demonstration of his attitude toward reason:

> who saw
> When this creation was? rememberst thou
> Thy making, while the Maker gave thee being?
> We know no time when we were not as now;
> Know none before us, self-begot, self-rais'd
> By our own quick'ning power, when fatal course
> Had circl'd his full Orbe.   (V, 856ff)

He is ridiculing the possibility of knowledge for Abdiel by setting
the fixed limits of knowledge within the self. If Abdiel was not
there it did not happen. If we do not know it then it is not so.
And seeing is believing. At least that is the limit to which reason
can be stretched for the opponent's mystery; it is strangely different when Satan announces his own version of the miracle of
creation.

Satan, of course, renders himself ridiculous by his argument.
As C. S. Lewis has commented, Satan both loses in dignity and
produces just the evidence to prove that he was not self-created.
It might be added that for the God he has rejected he must sup-
ply (besides the deity of self) an external power, Chance or Fate,
that is related to, and perhaps dependent upon still another power,
Time. One may observe that intellectually, more than physically,
Satan performs the office of rendering himself ridiculous, and
with a minimum of external assistance. This happens when his

materialistic bent of mind leads him to interpret having lasted one day of battle as proof of God's fallibility and nonomniscience. Since his position is often that of an opportunist, when he has to rationalize it he exposes himself.

But there is a certain amount of intellectual ridicule that is externally administered. For instance, a remark like this, which deliberately presents physical ridicule in terms of intellectual ridicule:

> that to be less then Gods
> Disdain'd, but meaner thoughts learnd in thir flight.
>
> (VI, 366f)

The two levels are joined again when the rebels are driven out of heaven; for we remember the initial slogan of freedom, later exalted to dominion, as they leave indiscriminately "together throngd," with even their own orders and degrees (which "Jarr not with liberty") beyond their concern. To be more accurate, this ridicule is not really administered externally. It is pointed up, by a kind of choral commentary, but it is already there, dramatically earned when the intellectual presumptions of the rebels work out their conflict with reality. This is true of the most important commentary on the intellectual ridiculousness of the rebels. It is the Son's remark before he unlooses the Father's indignation, and it goes to the very core of the rebels' position, to expose its essential incongruity — "mee they have despis'd, / Yet envied." They have envied His elevation, though by merit, and envied it in terms of might and in terms of scorn. The external ridicule only exposes what is internal, what in the course of dramatic action works its way out.

This is perhaps a convenient place to look back for a moment at Dr. Johnson's criticism, with which this study began. Milton, it is plain, like the metaphysical poets, and like other Renaissance writers, and like twentieth-century writers, has a much less restricted taste for incongruity than has Dr. Johnson. Milton, no less than Shakespeare or Donne, but in his own way, has a comprehensive taste for incongruity, which he can control and resolve into his larger structure. The "confusion of spirit and matter"

that Johnson deplored is controlled confusion, the dramatic working out of what Satan ignorantly set in motion.

But this is to jump a stage, for what we are supposed to be
considering still is the second level, that of mind. To pick up the
thread again, what is ridiculous about Satan's mind mostly reveals
itself by what he says and how, and by what he does. If his chief
use of reason is to destroy the authority of the reason, it is with
no intention of destroying the authority of the mind. The mind
is of great importance to Satan — the mind is its own place — but
that is because the mind has other faculties besides that of reason.

Satan's analysis of the first day's battle reveals a significant part
of his attitude toward the mind. We endured some disadvantage,
he admits, and pain, though as soon as we came to *know* that evil
we were able to be superior to it by despising it. Our "Empyreal
forme" is superior to wounds, which close and heal by our own
native vigor. The remedy of evil is as small as it is easy. Perhaps
"more valid Armes," more violent weapons will gain us superiority over our foes, or at least remove the odds they enjoyed,
since there is no essential difference between us in nature.

> if other hidden cause
> Left them Superiour, while we can preserve
> Unhurt our mindes, and understanding sound,
> Due search and consultation will disclose.   (VI, 442ff)

It is mind over matter; that is, the unconquerable will over material evil. It is also spiritual form that seems to be most prized for
its ability to resist, in a kind of material way, the material damage
of wounds. The mind must be preserved unhurt, like the spiritual
form, so that it can search out material means to gain a material
superiority. It is mind over matter but limited to matter, turned
downward to gain superiority on a lower plane, and running the
risk of adjusting to the plane upon which it has chosen to work
out its destiny.

In battle Satan's only moral quality is courage, a partial virtue
that has no moral value independent of other virtues. His chief
rational qualities are strength of will and inventive ingenuity. The
invention of artillery is a symbolic act, a characteristic achieve-

31

ment of Satan's mind (as Sin is), an achievement that exhibits Satan's great mastery over the material, and implies a reciprocal relationship between his mind and matter. Compared with him, his followers (apparently even Mammon) are superficial, surveying only the "bright surface" of things, with no "mind" for the materials underneath. But the significance of Satan's symbolic demonstration of mind over matter is not limited to himself; his act turns what has been a war conducted under discipline fatally toward chaos. To prevent general chaos, and to control the motion downward now inevitably begun, God's wrath must intervene, suspending free will so that heaven can ruin from heaven. To understand what is involved we must look at the key problem of discipline.

Satan's revolt is, among other things, a break in discipline. The best commentary comes from the encounter between Satan and Gabriel at the end of Book IV, an encounter, as we have observed, that provides an important commentary on the major themes of the war in heaven. Gabriel says:

> Was this your discipline and faith ingag'd,
> Your military obedience, to dissolve
> Allegeance to th' acknowledg'd Power supream?
>
> (IV, 954ff)

Whatever else it is, the break in discipline is a rational sin too, for Satan sets the stage for his revolt by depending upon the discipline upward of his inferiors, the while he is himself rejecting the discipline that he owes upward. His sin requires that his own allegiance be downward rather than upward for the external support necessary to any rational creature within the moral universe.

Milton's treatment of free will makes discipline a part of the rational soul (which traditionally comprehended both the understanding and the will). God requires obedience, but obedience freely given, an expression of the understanding carried out by the will. Adam's thoughts after having been created seem to be a demonstration of the reason (apparently natural reason) moving toward obedience:

how came I thus, how here?
Not of my self; by some great Maker then,
In goodness and in power praeeminent;
Tell me, how may I know him, how adore,
From whom I have that thus I move and live,
And feel that I am happier then I know.   (VIII, 277ff)

Contrasts this statement to that of Satan to Abdiel

Obedience must be freely given, but God helps His creatures perfect their wills. Ceremonies provide occasion in heaven, as on the day that "brings forth" heaven's Great Year, when the hosts are called by "Imperial summons." The orders and degrees provide every creature with opportunities for exercising his discipline: only God has no superior. Besides, the doing of disciplinary tasks is itself a ceremony in heaven. We remember that Raphael was sent on a ceremonial expedition to the gates of hell, and so was absent the day Adam was created:

> But us he sends upon his high behests
> For state, as Sovran King, and to enure
> Our prompt obedience.   (VIII, 238ff)

The Son, whose obedience is perfect, says that to obey the Father is "happiness entire." He says this as He assumes power on the third day of battle, in order to fulfill the divine will: only in this fulfillment does He have glory and exaltation. Meanwhile, the role of the loyal angels has been on a lower scale of fulfillment, closer to the performance of duty through the acceptance of discipline. Their service, which has been fearless and faithful, is accepted by God. This they are told by the Son; presumably their service includes, though unmentioned, the ridicule they suffered before Satan's cannon. (Abdiel had endured ridicule and "Universal reproach, far worse to beare / Then violence.") This physical ridicule, we must remember, is directly due to their arms; unarmed, Raphael comments, they could, as spirits, easily have evaded Satan's material missiles.

Why the arms? They make no literal sense, as Dr. Johnson readily saw, but they make the same kind of symbolic sense that the whole war makes. Are not the arms part of the limiting discipline, part of the ceremony of perfecting the will? Do not the arms limit the material might of both sides, to add to the limit which God has already providently set in order to prevent destruction? Actually, both sides are inconvenienced by their arms; for when the rebels are pinned under the mountains their armor helps trap them, crushing and bruising their "substance." For all his ingenuity, it does not occur to General Satan that his troops are really more powerful without the accepted discipline of their arms. The strategic lesson is learned only after Satan introduces a secret weapon that violates the code which he appears to be accepting and in fact partly is, though through ignorance. "Rage" prompts the loyal angels to counter-invention, which is superior to Satan's invention — perhaps because it breaks from the discipline altogether and returns more completely to fundamental material force. But it leads simply toward chaos, the destruction, not of the enemy, but of heaven. (There are literary overtones, for good measure, of Zeus' battle against the mountain-wielding forces of destruction, the Giants — in the hymn celebrating the creation Satan's rebels are significantly referred to as "the Giant Angels.") Finally, when the discipline has broken down, God suspends free will and intervenes:

> Warr wearied hath perform'd what Warr can do,
> And to disorder'd rage let loose the reines.   (VI, 695f)

But even the Chariot of God proceeds within the limits of discipline. It shakes all heaven — except the throne of God. And the Son checks half His strength, in order not to destroy.

There is plenty of evidence of Milton's personal interest in the problem of discipline; one pertinent commentary may be found in *Paradise Regained*, when Christ answers Satan's argument that God seeks glory. Christ replies that God made all only to show goodness freely; but, having done so, justly expects thanks:

> The slightest, easiest, readiest recompence
> From them who could return him nothing else,
> And not returning that would likeliest render
> Contempt instead, dishonour, obloquy.   (III, 128ff)

This is a version of traditional Elizabethan political philosophy, quite as applicable to the social structure or to the church structure (though Milton personally breaks with some of the implications). It is firmly based upon hierarchy; the discipline of order and degree expresses a philosophical view rather than mere etiquette, a philosophical view that regards order as possible only through discipline and therefore regards chaos as the logical alternative to discipline. Ulysses' great speech on "degree," in *Troilus and Cressida*, traces the steps leading to mere power and will and self-consuming appetite that finally ends in chaos. It is a significant commentary, but even more important for the circumstances under consideration is a pragmatic analysis by Bacon from his interpretation in *The Wisdom of the Ancients* of the myth of Orpheus. The myth is an image of philosophy — when Orpheus' music appeases the infernal powers it represents natural philosophy, when it attracts the beasts and trees it represents "Moral or Civil Discipline." Natural philosophy, Bacon says, with pointed wryness, is seldom or never attained:

And therefore Philosophy, hardly able to produce so excellent an Effect, in a pensive Humour (and not without cause), busies herself about Human Objects, and by Persuasion and Eloquence, insinuating the love of Virtue, Equity, and Concord in the Minds of Men, draws Multitudes of People to a Society, makes them subject to Laws, obedient to Government, and forgetful of their unbridled Affections, whilst they give Ear to Precepts, and submit themselves to Discipline; whence follows the building of Houses, erecting of Towns, planting of Fields and Orchards with Trees, and the like; insomuch that it would not be amiss to say, that even thereby Stones and Woods were called together and settled in Order. . . . Tumults and Seditions and Wars arise; in the midst of which Hurly-burlies, first Laws are silent, Men return to the pravity of their Natures; Fields and Towns are wasted and depopulated; and then (if their Fury continue) Learning and Philosophy must needs be dismembered; so that a few Fragments only, and in some Places, will be found like the scattered Boards of Shipwreck, so as a barbarous Age must follow.

The material sin is punished most completely during the war, and in a material way. The sins against mind and spirit receive

35

their full punishment only over a longer period of time; the punishment is also in kind, by internal development, through degeneration. But the material is the thread that runs through the other two levels, for Raphael's basic metaphor was to express divine happenings by likening spiritual to corporeal forms. For the critic trying to express what happens in the poem perhaps another metaphor may be used, that of the circle, which is a traditional symbol of the divine; but if the circle expresses the impostor divine, it is a symbol of moral irony and the ridiculous.

The break in discipline presumes completeness within the circle of self. When Satan declares that his puissance is his own, he is denying the possibility of a source of power external to himself. He is also referring inward to self for moral sanction, rather than outward. He is declaring that he is, or can be, at the top of the hierarchy, the one uncircumscribed circle. If he is not right, then he has tried to ascend the scale of creation by an internal willing of self God. The orthodox method of ascent, as Raphael tells Adam, is by being nearer or tending nearer to God: which means rising toward a purer resignation in His will, which is always external to the creature.

To make self an impostor god means trying to possess the power of spirit by means of matter. One might almost say by grace of matter, for the elevation of self to godhead may require taking matter into a partnership of deity. Not that matter is without worth — the concept of a scale of creation implies the value of matter and the possibility of ascent. Milton himself is very firm on the indivisibility of flesh and spirit. Raphael's metaphor of spiritual in corporeal form is also a way of explaining, by an earthly analogue in terms of matter, what is otherwise unexplainable in human terms — the hierarchy of spirit which works upward by merit, that closest to God being "more spiritous." Matter, both real and metaphorical, does not lack dignity. But Satan confounds the material with the external; in his search for power external to himself he turns to the material, which he thinks he can master with his mind, and so make part of his own puissance.

The invention of artillery is an attempt to usurp ultimate moral might by means of matter:

> eternal might
> To match with thir inventions they presum'd
> So easie, and of his Thunder made a scorn.   (VI, 630ff)

It is setting matter against spirit by means of mind. And matter that can ascend by spirit can also descend, if spirit breaks its discipline and tends further from the source of its informing power.

Ultimate moral law and ultimate force *are* external, but to be confused with material force only by the morally perverted. Through free will, if God allows an equal contest and sends only one third of His angels against the rebel third, perverse will can cause a deadlock that requires the intervention of external power. But the external power fulfills moral law and only completes the circle that has been ignorantly set in motion.

A NOTE ON HELL

In HELL the broad and powerful effects that make the major impressions are the effects of defiance and achievement. But these play against a small and telling counterpoint. If we remember only the bold effects, or if we discount them logically or historically, we are abstracting separate themes that have their full meaning only in the total context of their development.

There are early intimations that hell is not static. The first occurs when Satan, still prone on the flood, observes that the sulphurous hail "oreblown" has laid the "fiery Surge," and that thunder "Perhaps hath spent his shafts." The second occurs when Satan moves from the liquid fire to the solid fire of the dry plain. His steps over the "burning Marle" are painful; nevertheless, "he so endur'd." To a Nisroc pain may be the worst of all evils; but to a Satan, who proclaims his will unconquerable and his mind superior to place, pain is not final hell — not so long as he still feels his mind to have power over matter, and can prove that power by being able to act himself and by being able to project that power into the minds of his followers. He rouses his troops, first by harsh sarcasm and then by a strangely anachronistic appeal to their military fear. The conqueror beholds you with your arms scattered, he says; and will "anon"

discern
Th' advantage, and descending tread us down
Thus drooping.   (I, 326ff)

38

The treading down and the drooping describe their state, we discover later, before the chariot of the Lord. Here the statement seems only the normal precaution of a good leader; in addition, the statement, and its rousing effect, implies that the defeat was not total and that the conflict is continuing. Satan, by a violent act of assertive will, is denying the past and forcing an unconscious agreement from his followers long before the infernal debate in Pandemonium will make this position official. Satan's will prevails, as it did over Beelzebub's realization that God may have left them their spirit and strength "Strongly to suffer and support our pains." The defeat is perforce admitted, but in terms of equal, dubious battle finally lost to superior weapons — the kind of defeat that does not seem to prohibit thinking about a future.

The most nearly accurate version of the catastrophe in heaven is Belial's; but this, like his praise of God's power, is partly discredited by the context, and Milton is willing to contribute to the ambiguity of Belial's account by pointing up Belial's motives. (Needless to say, Milton does not do this in order to favor Satan's heroic energy.) Belial sums up the progress that has already been made in hell, and, therefore, what there is to lose:

> is this then worst
> Thus sitting, thus consulting, thus in Arms?   (II, 163f)

It was worse when we were being struck by thunder, he says; hell seemed a refuge then; it was worse when we were chained on the burning lake; it could be still worse. If the fallen angels do not experience the kind of hell Belial describes, it is because there are other plans made for them.

That hell is external to the mind is made sufficiently clear — in spite of the apparent import of Satan's ambiguous boast. That was delivered in private, to Beelzebub. Satan's public position is that "this Infernal Pit shall never hold / Caelestial Spirits in Bondage." This last seems deliberately ambiguous, leaving room as it does for remaining in hell but free. What immediately follows also rings with declamatory defiance but has a cooler secondary meaning: "nor th' Abysse / Long under darkness cover." It sounds as if they will be getting out from under darkness, but it may be that they will just improve the lighting. A little later, when Satan is opening the debate, he has progressed, by no discernible logic, from the "shall never hold":

> For since no deep within her gulf can hold
> Immortal vigor, though opprest and fall'n,
> I give not Heav'n for lost.   (II, 12ff)

Similarly he has progressed from his private declaration (to Beelzebub) of "eternal" war, which can only mean resistance with no hope of victory, to his public statement of optimism:

> For who can yet beleeve, though after loss,
> That all these puissant Legions, whose exile
> Hath emptied Heav'n, shall faile to re-ascend
> Self-rais'd, and repossess their native seat.   (I, 631ff)

What the weaker angels desire is to make the mind its own place:

> To found this nether Empire, which might rise
> By pollicy, and long process of time,
> In emulation opposite to Heav'n.   (II, 296ff)

This is a concept of hell allowed by free will. (And Satan, though he may provide us with some interesting dramatic demonstrations, cannot yet entirely realize the extent to which hell will be in his mind.) Beelzebub is spokesman for Satan's more considered view, which is a compromise one that sets as goal not the reconquest of heaven but escape and opportunistic raids. Instead of trying to hatch vain empires in hell, which *is* a dungeon, under the "inevitable curb" of God's jurisdiction, the plan is to make hell a base of operations. At worst, hell will be a place to retire to with conquests and spoils and revenge; at best, it will be the base for successful conquest of the earth and man, "Nor will occasion want" for "advantagious act . . . By sudden onset." The externality is again strongly emphasized, and the more desirable policy of escaping rather than adjusting, when Beelzebub speaks of returning nearer to heaven:

> perhaps in view
> Of those bright confines, whence with neighbouring Arms

And opportune excursion we may chance
Re-enter Heav'n; or else in some milde Zone
Dwell not unvisited of Heav'ns fair Light
Secure, and at the brightning Orient beam
Purge off this gloom; the soft delicious Air,
To heal the scarr of these corrosive Fires
Shall breathe her balme.   (II, 394ff)

That is the line official policy takes, which does not accept the mind as its own place and is not content to build upon the psychological and material progress that has been made in hell. But the unofficial policy, into the workings of which we have had some glimpses, also continues.

The fallen angels proceed with their efforts to make a heaven of hell. Though at last free, they continue to imitate the ceremonies of rank and state that they learned in heaven, but not without some significant additions of sultanic pomp. Though hell is formally democratic, the same hierarchy that prevailed in heaven is held to. In fact, the differences in state are strikingly pointed up, as they never were in heaven. During the debate in Pandemonium the "great Seraphic Lords" sit in secret conclave, and "in thir own dimensions like themselves"; but the humble followers who crowd the gates, porches, and hall are reduced to smallest size — the similes indicate, along with other suggestions by overtones, that they are like bees or elves.

The anonymous fallen angels, who begin by being astonished on the oblivious pool, are recuperated as beings under discipline, and make their initial attempt to regain their lost heavenly state by means of martial ceremony. Heavenly state is imitated by the morale-building pomp of the military review. At first the fallen spring up like surprised sentries, partly numbed still, but not without awareness:

Nor did they not perceave the evil plight
In which they were, or the fierce pains not feel.   (I, 335f)

They obey "their great Sultan," and come pouring in haste, innumerable as locusts or the barbarians of the North — but still military only in their obedience. And after the epic roll call, when

their interrupted advance is again returned to, they are still un-
elevated, dependent even for motion and direction upon the superior will of Satan: "All these and more came flocking." But
Satan, after he gently raises their courage with "high words,"
orders a military review that puts them through motions resembling their former state. It is all excessively magnificent, the splen-
dor and elevation of heaven imitated by the fallen — desperately
superficial. Satan's ensign

> Shon like a Meteor streaming to the Wind
> With Gemms and Golden lustre rich imblaz'd,
> Seraphic arms and Trophies: all the while
> Sonorous mettal blowing Martial sounds.   (I, 537ff)

Satan significantly cultivates pomp in hell:

> Mean while the winged Haralds by command
> Of Sovran power, with awful Ceremony
> And Trumpets sound throughout the Host proclaim
> A solemn Councel forthwith to be held
> At *Pandaemonium*, the high Capital
> Of Satan and his Peers.   (I, 752ff)

And after the lofty exchange of hell's best opinions in formal
council, in which Satan's role is that of shrewd manipulation from
behind the scenes, the great decision must be announced with
ceremony befitting hell's version of heaven:

> The *Stygian* Councel thus dissolv'd; and forth
> In order came the grand infernal Peers,
> Midst came thir mighty Paramount, and seemd
> Alone th' Antagonist of Heav'n, nor less
> Then Hells dread Emperour with pomp Supream,
> And God-like imitated State; him round
> A Globe of fierie Seraphim inclos'd
> With bright imblazonrie, and horrent Arms.
> Then of thir Session ended they bid cry
> With Trumpets regal sound the great result:
> Toward the four winds four speedy Cherubim
> Put to thir mouths the sounding Alchymie
> By Haralds voice explain'd: the hollow Abyss
> Heard farr and wide, and all the host of Hell

With deafning shout, return'd them loud acclaim.
Thence more at ease thir minds . . . (II, 506ff)

It is a magnificent piece of epic mockery, a tissue of the heightened, the overheightened, the deliberately ambiguous, and the
amusedly detached. The official policy is echoed when Satan
seems alone to be the antagonist of heaven. But the unofficial policy, of making a heaven of hell, is presented more strongly — by
the mischievous anticlimax of the "nor less" than the emperor of
hell, and by the demonstration of the infernal pomp supreme pay-
ing its ignorant tribute to heaven with bright show and sounding
alchemy. *ans. to ❦ A.J.A. Wal-*
dock
  Pandemonium is perhaps the most significant example of the
unofficial policy unwittingly pursuing its symbolic expression. *and*
Pandemonium imitates glory materially. Magnificence is possible, *M. M.*
which draws praise for the work or for the architect; but the *Ross*
magnificence does not lead the beholder's mind anywhere else, at
least not upward. The effect is rather that of pleasure with the
ingenuity of hell, and a sense of accommodation that is to take
the place of elevation. The most significant detail is the indoor
lighting, "As from a sky."
  The fallen mind that is here trying to be its own place is a
materialistic mind, and so its conscious imitations of heaven are
naively materialistic. Mammon, with his practical extension of
Belial's platform, is the chief spokesman for the unofficial policy.
We can imitate heaven's light, he declares, just as God sometimes
imitates hell when He covers His throne with the majesty of darkness. We have gems and gold here, and we are not lacking in skill
or art. We can raise "Magnificence; and what can Heav'n shew
more?" Mammon's policy is active and creative, but the sphere
is rigidly limited: the whole range of creative activity is reduced
to the circle of self within the circle of hell. Mammon's is a *practical* decision, in which mind comes to terms with the arguments
of place: "Compose our present evils, with regard / Of what we
are and where." A substitute heaven will be erected out of the
partnership of mind and place. Good will be sought from self
("Our own good from our selves"); good will be sought from the

43

environment; they will, with God-like imitated moral law, bring good out of evil. That is what part of it sounds like, but Mammon is not really interested in moral states and does not carry through with his idea of imitation. His language reveals his range of interest: "Our greatness will appear / Then most conspicuous." And it develops that their bringing good out of evil really means *thriving* under evil by adjusting entirely to place: "Our torments also may in length of time / Become our elements." It is the practical decision of a complete materialist who is maintaining that paradise is within if only the external sanction of environment can be won.

agrees with C.S. Lewis

Pandemonium, sports, song, philosophy — these can suspend hell, can charm, excite, arm; but hell remains hell, a comprehensive wilderness that seems to permit, for an uncertain time and an uncertain designation of place, the illusion of frontier. Within the illusion they may follow Satan's advice (delivered emotionally to contrast with his own bold hard lot):

> intend at home,
> While here shall be our home, what best may ease
> The present misery, and render Hell
> More tollerable; if there be cure or charm
> To respite or deceive, or slack the pain
> Of this ill Mansion: intermit no watch
> Against a wakeful Foe, while I abroad
> Through all the coasts of dark destruction seek
> Deliverance for us all.   (II, 457ff)

That is the official version of the relationship between mind and place. But outside the area where some material superiority seems to have been gained over place by mind lies the classic hell with all its static horrors.

There the waters of Lethe offer forgetfulness to any of the fallen who can swallow a drop. And the damned try, we are told; they try to reach the water as they are being ferried across for arbitrary punishment "At certain revolutions." Not now, for this is only the casual background of a dateless future that is momentarily explored while the real explorers, in the immediate present, make their first extensive survey of hell, and while the chief ex-

44

plorer, Satan, makes his first expedition, not unconnected with the
dateless future, to earth. The casual background contradicts, by a
powerful incongruity that is not without the trace of a smile, both
official and unofficial policy. Hell *is* ultimately real and external
— not just a base for operations elsewhere, and not to be turned
into a materialistic heaven either by an act of will (Satan's) or by
an act of salesmanship (Mammon's) that makes mind a partner
of place by becoming place. That is not sufficient oblivion for the
damned mind; it wants Lethe.

The free will allowed evil makes possible the continuance of
the conflict. But since evil cannot harm God, ultimately it can
harm only itself, and every outward success is an inward failure.
The conflict, therefore, is no real conflict but a show conducted
on a stage from which it is impossible for the fallen actors to escape the perspective of irony. The war in heaven, though conducted as a war, is beneath the surface a conflict in ironies. It is
the kind of conflict that the Milton of the prose wars can conduct
very well.

The unconquerable will that is in a hopeless position can express
power in irony, and so admit some of the truth of the hopelessness
while maintaining a kind of unyielding superiority through laughter. And the mind that asserts it is its own place can, backed by
the will and disdain, assert its mastery over situation:

> Farewel happy Fields
> Where Joy for ever dwells: Hail horrours, hail
> Infernal world, and thou profoundest Hell
> Receive thy new Possessor.   (I, 249ff)

Through irony the "fixt mind" can at least mock the creator of
the situation:

> Here at least
> We shall be free; th' Almighty hath not built
> Here for his envy, will not drive us hence.   (I, 258ff)

When his fellows are involved Satan is likely to use a broader and
more direct mockery that is closer to sarcasm, but indirectly it

may also defy the situation — as when he rouses his followers from the burning lake.

Satan's irony, then, is a characteristic expression of his will, of his selfness:

> What matter where, if I be still the same,
> And what I should be.   (I, 256f)

If a point can be gained for the will, the self may seem to be sacrificed temporarily; but that is only a trick, for Satan's real self resides only in the will, is indivisible from will. "Fall'n Cherube," Satan says to Beelzebub, and gives us a fine example of his irony, apparently human in its expression of superiority through inclusion of self — like some of the subtle effects a Negro can get by calling himself or another Negro "nigger." But there is no humorous complexity in Satan's inclusion of self; he is using himself to provide leverage for his will, to gain mastery in an immediate situation.

"Let us not slip th' occasion." That is Satan's comment as he marks the cease of the sulphurous hail and thunder and characteristically resolves to take advantage of the situation — "whether scorn / Or satiate fury yield it from our Foe." Great villain that he is (one is tempted, in the search for an adequate phrase, to call him tragic villain), he is a master of opportunism, and is charmed into being slave to what he is master of; because the irony of moral law encompasses and turns against itself the irony that can be brought to bear by the individual will. One might say that Satan's irony is verbal and gives him at best an opportunistic mastery of the moment. It always turns out to have been rooted in the moment rather than in reality. For instance, his turning things topsy-turvy against Abdiel and calling him seditious angel. Part of Abdiel's reply, "Reign thou in Hell thy Kingdom, let mee serve / In Heav'n," Satan ignorantly echoes in one of the bravura passages that display, and for the time achieve, a kind of mastery over hell — "Better to reign in Hell, then serve in Heav'n."

Sometimes the verbal mastery of situation seems close to superficial word-play, as in the public rhetoric of "Surer to prosper then prosperity / Could have assur'd us." At other times the mastery may come from making a moral truth fit the occasion: "who overcomes / By force, hath overcome but half his foe." Always it is the will expressing itself, balancing upon the gain of the moment, putting the future to the same risk as the past. But irony, the will's great instrument for mastering the moment, cannot be confined to the moment. Perhaps one might even say that it is the power of being outside the moment that gives irony power over the moment. When Satan declares that evil shall be his good, he is asserting a logical paradox that makes it possible for him to carry on, since he is not pure evil but fallen, and therefore dependent upon a concept of moral good outside himself. It is the technique of calling Abdiel a seditious angel, to raise a laugh that consciously involves the self in order to gain the moment. Although the laugh and the paradox indicate ironic awareness that is not limited to the immediate situation, still ironic awareness is not static; degree and the extent of control determine ultimate mastery. Satan's control does not go far.

In Satan's "fixt mind" and "high disdain" and "unconquerable Will" (which Satan asserts are his positive inner qualities, in contrast to the change he admits in his "outward lustre"), we are seeing the circle of God's irony, which always encompasses Satan's. His whole recorded career is example, but let us look at one significant instance, his opening of the consultation in hell. He sits exalted,

> by merit rais'd
> To that bad eminence; and from despair
> Thus high uplifted beyond hope, aspires
> Beyond thus high.   (II, 5ff)

This introduction represents an irony, as from a chorus, that Satan cannot control very far, but still he exploits it for the moment. He extends his earlier mockery — that at least they will be free in hell since the Almighty has not built here for His envy — into an opportunistic position. They will have the advantage of union without faction, he says, for no one will enviously claim precedence in hell, to acquire a greater share of pain or a rank closer the thunder. The immediate result of this position is to reassert his claim to eminence by reason of his superior will.

C. S. Lewis, in reducing Satan's argument to its illogical nonsense, seems to overlook the possibility that Satan may be conscious of what he is saying. It seems to me that Satan is relishing his ironic wit and expecting his followers to recognize the performance as proof of his mastery over the immediate situation, for he is managing to laugh at it while making his limited political point. But beyond the bitter joke of the moment and the political advantage, the irony is not in Satan's control at all. Except for the quick opportunistic laugh he is the complete subject of the irony, raised by merit beyond hope, and using his supremacy of will to conceal from them his supreme misery.

One source of Satan's great power of will and motion is despair. Before the chariot of God he and his followers were able to conceive hope from despair and so harden the more. That is God's announced punishment for evil, the perverse internal strengthening that makes possible the progressive self-destruction, that allows great power of motion without control of direction, and so constitutes the real death of the will while evil ignorantly punishes itself and produces good. The angel chorus that celebrates the creation of the world tells of the irony which is moral law:

> Who seekes
> To lessen thee, against his purpose serves
> To manifest the more thy might: his evil
> Thou usest, and from thence creat'st more good.
>
> (VII, 613ff)

In heaven Satan had wagered all on power and was paid in kind. His petty invention of artillery received its first answer from the inventive rage of the loyal angels (the mountain-throwing constitutes a similar, but more destructive, break in discipline) and its final answer from the chariot of God.

Satan's invention of artillery is so characteristic a product of his mind that the metaphor of recoil becomes elevated to a symbol. It is the metaphor that sums up his revolt:

> but the evil soon
> Driv'n back redounded as a flood on those
> From whom it sprung, impossible to mix
> With Blessedness. (VII, 56ff)

It is the metaphor God uses when He first calls attention to Satan's escape from hell:

> so bent he seems
> On desperat revenge, that shall redound
> Upon his own rebellious head. (III, 84ff)

The choral opening of Book IV repeats the metaphor: "And like a devellish Engine back recoiles / Upon himself." And Satan accepts the image in the soliloquy that follows his return to Eden involved in a rising mist:

> the more I see
> Pleasures about me, so much more I feel
> Torment within me, as from the hateful siege
> Of contraries; all good to me becomes
> Bane, and in Heav'n much worse would be my state.
> But neither here seek I, no nor in Heav'n
> To dwell, unless by maistring Heav'ns Supreame;
> Nor hope to be my self less miserable
> By what I seek, but others to make such
> As I, though thereby worse to me redound;
> For onely in destroying I finde ease
> To my relentless thoughts. (IX, 119ff)

And again, a few lines later:

> Revenge, at first though sweet,
> Bitter ere long back on it self recoiles;
> Let it; I reck not. (IX, 171ff)

The inner evil is forced to seek outward expression and so close the circle upon itself. Free will leaves him free to act, the inner hardness provides unrelenting drive to the opportunism that shrewdly seeks the point of maximum penetration: which is also the point of ultimate self-defeat.

We have already touched upon many of the separate ironies that make up the larger irony of Satan proceeding, whatever the stage of his consciousness, under the direction of God's will, pursuing the necessary evil that is his good. Tortured by partial awareness, he seeks to destroy all good, but is still subject to good, for he too is fallen. Though he founds everything on self, he is forced to depend on values outside himself. They are always secondary values that recoil, like the loyalty to his followers that turns into the moral circle of his dependence upon their dependence; or his responding to Eve's beauty, but feeling the terror in it; or his feeling pity that turns, in spite of and because of his unconquerable will, into self-pity.

The larger irony requires a dramatic hell, one that is external to the fallen and for a time partly subject to their will, one that is not merely a state of mind but nevertheless maintains a significant relationship with state of mind. So Beelzebub is not entirely wrong in his crudely materialistic analysis: what if their conqueror has left them their strength and spirit only to "do him mightier service" and "Strongly to suffer and support our pains"? Satan, though he has no superior in materialism, also has greater moral understanding than any of his followers. He knows that the conflict is between good and evil, and that God will not merely exact service and suffering, but will try to exact good from their evil. He sees that clearly, and he sees much else in fits and starts, but his will owes no small amount of its power to its blindness. Beelzebub, raised from his miserable weakness, assumes unfalteringly the role of Satan's political lieutenant. But what Beelzebub says in his first weak speech, though crude in its range of awareness, is part of Satan's consciousness too. Satan knows all that, and much more. It is in his consciousness that he approaches tragedy perhaps enough to be called a tragic villain. None of his followers has so clear an awareness that hell is both internal and external:

> Which way I flie is Hell; my self am Hell;
> And in the lowest deep a lower deep
> Still threatning to devour me opens wide,
> To which the Hell I suffer seems a Heav'n.   (IV, 75ff)

Yet the followers whom Satan leads also lead him, and there are significant relationships in personality as well as consciousness. For all his limitations, including his scorn of wiles, Moloch is an essential part of Satan, the Satan of the "fixt mind" and absolute physical courage, unafraid of Death. So is Belial, in spite of the obvious differences, a part of Satan — Belial the orator and seducer, with the soothing fullness and soft fall of his periods; the sensuous optimist and the shrewd psychologist; the materialistic professor of mind as motion; the prophet of mind becoming place (Satan's phrase modified by Belial's interpretation, and by events); the interpreter of Satan's "to be weak is miserable / Doing or Suffering":

> To suffer, as to doe,
> Our strength is equal. (II, 199f)

And Mammon, especially, is part of Satan. If Mammon taught man, he had a master in Satan. The invention of artillery is but one example. The Satan who declares that evil will be his good is, like Mammon, seeking his own good from himself, and coming to final terms with environment. The Mammon who proposes to thrive "Through labour and endurance" seems to be echoing Satan's doing or suffering. And his equating heaven with magnificence — "what can Heav'n shew more?" — is more than a verbal echo of Satan's early defiance, "And what is else not to be overcome?"

But finally, though these followers are only fragments of Satan, they lead him as he leads them. They quietly assume his powerful articulation, "The mind is its own place," and turn it into the unofficial policy of making a heaven of hell. And Satan is caught in the drift, made to accept the heaven of hell in spite of the official policy of making hell only a base of operations. He says nothing directly about the issue, but adjusts. He admits that he is himself hell, he confesses his need for the actual hell when he complains about the hateful siege of contraries in Eden, and he is accepting both the real externality of hell (an object to which he is subject) and his own adjustment when he thinks of the ultimate hell that threatens him: "To which the Hell I suffer seems a Heav'n."

THE GARDEN

WE FIRST approach the happy Garden from the Fall. Immediately outside this "happy rural seat of various view" is the impassable wilderness — steep, hairy, overgrown, grotesque, wild, denying access; the trees that rise in ascent are of insuperable height; beneath them all is steep and savage, entwined, tangling, perplexing. That seems to be part of the various view, though outside. It is presented with an intensity of detail and sustained frustration, then interrupted by a glimpse and a *sense* of Paradise, then returned to with a varied repetition that changes nothing, except the tightness of our expectations. It has become so much a part of the experience of entering the Garden that it enters with us; we bring the outside, at least as vivid memory, into the more vivid inside. And if the entrance into Paradise is — as it must be for fallen man — a return, then we bring a recent immediate memory of the outside into our ancient memory of the inside.

Stretching beyond, from the prospect provided by the Tree of Life and the great narrative office behind everything we see, are the famous realms that make history after the Fall and acquire their fame then. Our immediate guide through the wonders of the Garden is leviathan-explorer-merchant-griffin-vulture-scout-wolf-cormorant-Satan, fresh from the wonders of hell and his mind still enough its own place. For a long moment he is a tourist against his will, gaping in admiration at what is before him. Behind him are the wonders of hell, the other extreme of the natural

world, an extreme that man can approach only through the imagination, an extreme that is ultimately inexpressible but can be approached by myth and metaphor:

> O're many a Frozen, many a Fierie Alpe,
> Rocks, Caves, Lakes, Fens, Bogs, Dens, and shades of death,
> A Universe of death, which God by curse
> Created evil, for evil only good,
> Where all life dies, death lives, and nature breeds,
> Perverse, all monstrous, all prodigious things,
> Abominable, inutterable, and worse
> Then Fables yet have feign'd, or fear conceiv'd,
> *Gorgons* and *Hydra's*, and *Chimera's* dire.   (II, 620ff)

Behind him is that infernal marvel of imagination, Pandemonium,
the best that could be made out of the worst, the metropolis-oasis
in the desert, infernal paradise.

So this is our first view of the Garden, through the eyes and
the experienced history of the first fall, which is linked to and
anticipates the second. From the perspective of Satan and from
our own, that of fallen humanity, we experience an archetypal
state that cannot be known to us directly. It can be known only
through the metaphorical creation of an image that will awaken
our memories (in a Jungian sense; or, to bring the concept closer
to Milton, in the Neoplatonic sense that memory is the province
of the soul). Since the created image is just that, a metaphor and
not an absolute mystic vision, it must proceed by the normal
processes of creation, through opposites — through our mixed experience of impure and pure states, through our muffled and fitful
intuitions of a pure state, through contrast and conflict. The situation requires the poet to be mythic, to create an image of the
archetype for us; but the situation forbids that he do it naively,
protects him from having to do so: or rather he has created, in
the situation, his own protective dramatic structure. It is an *image*
of the archetype that he creates, a symbolic image in a dramatic
situation that helps create the image and protect it at once — protect it by maintaining the ultimate impossibility of the *image* of
the real archetype.

shades of Jung

Back of the image is the known cultural history — *Gan Eden* as historical fact. Related is the pagan tradition of the Golden Age, recorded in myth and literature, in political and legal theory. Related is the tradition of pastoral poetry, which came to be written by town poets. Related is the occasional human yearning for peace and quiet, for an impossibly ideal Arcadia where wilderness may be thought paradise enow; or there is the desire to withdraw from complexity, from "the fury and mire of human veins," to withdraw even, especially, from the self and its involvements; or there are the claims of childhood, at least the golden moments of childhood, symbolized (along with much more) by the persistent "archetype of the child." And always a sense of impossibility, which is part of the inevitable impurity that makes the pure vision so terribly intense.

In the Hebrew story *Gan Eden* is no Arcadia, no place of retirement, but from the beginning a place of trial. Discipline, complexity (however simple it may seem to the sophisticated descendants of Adam), a concept of self — these are original necessities that are contemporaneous with human bliss in its purest original: which must mean as pure as could be. For Christians influenced by Platonic and Neoplatonic thought, as for Philo Judaeus, the presence of Eve in the Garden would indicate the impossibility of pure direct knowledge of the One.

> But 'twas beyond a mortal's share
> To wander solitary there:
> Two paradises 'twere in one
> To live in Paradise alone.

The doctrine of original sin and the accumulated tradition expressing man's need to return, as far as he could, toward the primary cause by strenuously trying to understand secondary causes — this would require the Garden's being understood symbolically, as a place impossible to return to in the flesh.

It is important to emphasize from the first that Milton's Garden is no expression, however refined, of crude wish-fulfillment. Milton does not "abandon" himself in his descriptions; he is not engaged in a sentimental game of remolding the world nearer to the

54

heart's desire. The artist's discipline, which does not fail him elsewhere, does not fail him here.

These are general observations, by way of preface. Let us
return to Satan's first entrance into Paradise. The brief invocation-
prologue to Book IV gives us two views of Satan — the conventional "now first inflam'd with rage," and the ironic "Yet not
rejoycing in his speed, though bold, / Far off and fearless." Conscience wakes despair and the

> bitter memorie
> Of what he was, what is, and what must be
> Worse. (IV, 24ff)

We have a figurative use of *memory*, which can be awakened to
the past; or even to the present (through the agency of *conscience*-understanding), the *real* present that seems part of the
past because it unhappily is (it *was* no dream), and because one
has been awakened to it; or awakened even to the future, because
the future that can be anticipated and yet is accepted as inevitable
has become a conscious part of the past, and so, fitly, part of the
torture of memory. The paradox is a witty exploration of the
level of consciousness that lies under the joyless speed. Satan re-
coils upon himself, caught, in the memory of what he is, between
the double sense of what he was (in heaven and in hell) and what
he will be. The immediate past-present is hell, the immediate
present-future is Paradise: Satan is caught there, between the remote past, not to be known again, of heaven and the remote
future, the threatening "lower deep" that he cannot finally know
until God's appointed time. He is also caught, in a physical sense
that has its overtones, between heaven and Eden:

> Sometimes towards *Eden* which now in his view
> Lay pleasant, his grievd look he fixes sad,
> Sometimes towards Heav'n and the full-blazing Sun,
> Which now sat high in his Meridian Towre:
> Then much revolving, thus in sighs began. (IV, 27ff)

It is a brilliant setting of the dramatic scene; Satan temporarily
breaks under the pressure, and in the long soliloquy that follows
faces as much of the truth as he can.

Satan patches his outward self together again over the excision of hope, fear, and original good: "Each perturbation smooth'd with outward calme." He proceeds again toward Eden, after the long interruption for self-inventory. What seemed generally pleasant from a distance receives no further specific notice until he is almost there, for apparently his mind is on other things:

> So on he fares, and to the border comes
> Of *Eden*, where delicious Paradise,
> Now nearer, Crowns with her enclosure green,
> As with a rural mound the champain head
> Of a steep wilderness, whose hairie sides
> With thicket overgrown, grottesque and wilde,
> Access deni'd. (IV, 131ff)

C. S. Lewis has justly observed that the sequence of Satan's entering Paradise resembles a dream. There is the detailed perception of frustrating obstacles that reveal themselves mounting level upon level. Then, after a sense of Paradise and a digression, we are back faced with the very nearest of the obstacles; but it was all wrong, for the one gate is on the other side. And that does not matter anyway, for Satan contemptuously leaps over the total barrier. I should want to add that the dream has qualities reminiscent of an archetypal return. More important than the implications of the "hairie sides" (which Mr. Lewis apparently accepts) is the sense of the real-unreal, the sense of being in a dreamed experience that has truth in it but is not simple translatable truth. The vision is not a pure mystic vision in which identity is lost, for a sense of doubleness is permitted, and surprise, and even deception. Perhaps one should say it is a human groping toward a purely intuitive archetypal return, a groping that is not quite pure but maintains elements of self-consciousness. The highest obstacle of all divides and reverses part of the emotional direction, for it turns out to be the inviting fruit-laden trees of Paradise. And this sense of doubleness, of a view descending from Paradise, related to the ascending view but miraculously independent, like a kind of musical crab canon, is established by the penultimate obstacle, the "verdurous wall":

Which to our general Sire gave prospect large
Into his neather Empire neighbouring round.   (IV, 144f)

(Note that *we* are definitely included here, as we really have been all along, and not just Satan as a solitary agent.) What immediately follows, about the landscape, further develops the view within, as if we were already entered.

The whole passage, in its doubleness, in its dreamed return, is remarkably like (for reasons more fundamental than literary "imitation") the remembered vision of "our first world" in Eliot's "Burnt Norton":

Footfalls echo in the memory
Down the passage which we did not take
Towards the door we never opened
Into the rose-garden . . .
                    shall we follow
The deception of the thrush? Into our first world.
There they were, dignified, invisible,
Moving without pressure, over the dead leaves,
In the autumn heat, through the vibrant air,
And the bird called, in response to
The unheard music hidden in the shrubbery,
And the unseen eyebeam crossed, for the roses
Had the look of flowers that are looked at.
There they were as our guests, accepted and accepting.
So we moved, and they, in a formal pattern . . .

And some of these qualities of the dreamed return – the apparently difficult approach and the self-conscious doubleness – are essential in Faulkner's tale of paradise lost, "The Bear":

. . . he saw the wilderness through a slow drizzle of November rain just above the ice point as it seemed to him later he always saw it or at least always remembered it – the tall and endless wall of dense November woods under the dissolving afternoon and the year's death, sombre, impenetrable (he could not even discern yet how, at what point they could possibly hope to enter it even though he knew that Sam Fathers was waiting there with the wagon) . . . until, dwarfed by that perspective into an almost ridiculous diminishment, the surrey itself seemed to have ceased to move.

We return to Satan from the landscape within Paradise; or rather, with the marvelous outdoing itself, Paradise comes to meet him:

> And of pure now purer aire
> Meets his approach, and to the heart inspires
> Vernal delight and joy, able to drive
> All sadness but despair: now gentle gales
> Fanning thir odoriferous wings dispense
> Native perfumes, and whisper whence they stole
> Those balmie spoiles. As when to them who saile
> Beyond the *Cape of Hope,* and now are past
> *Mozambic,* off at Sea North-East windes blow
> *Sabean* Odours from the spicie shoare
> Of *Arabie* the blest, with such delay
> Well pleas'd they slack thir course, and many a League
> Cheard with the grateful smell old Ocean smiles.
> So entertaind those odorous sweets the Fiend
> Who came thir bane.   (IV, 153ff)

This too includes more than Satan. The air inspires joy to *the* heart. But no matter how luxuriously, and innocently, the description seems to wander, it never ceases to explore the drama of Satan's consciousness. The "joy" is a small echo of the speed he has not been rejoicing in. The air that can "drive" any sadness except "despair" reawakens the echo of the "conscience" that awoke slumbering despair. In effect it is like the philosophy in hell that could "charm" for a while, or the harmony that could suspend hell and ravish the audience, or like the Dorian marching music that could charm their painful steps and "chase" (also for a while) "Anguish and doubt and fear and sorrow and pain." The gentle breezes "dispense" the perfumes, a word that is perhaps excessive for a mere natural act, and may suggest the larger dispensation of Providence which this act reflects (as the sun's lordly eye "Dispenses Light from farr"); and may suggest, torturingly, the large "Act of Grace" that Satan had for a moment considered as a possibility. The breezes are not content with smelling, but "whisper" their account of the order of dispensation, and do so in terms that significantly reflect Satan's mind. They tell "whence they stole / Those balmie spoiles." And so they at once reflect the order of dispensation, and betray Satan's intended crime as the "first grand Thief," and anticipate Satan's own language when he says that man has been endowed "With Heav'nly spoils, our spoils."

Then there is the luxurious epic simile, traditionally digressive, wantoning in rich description, with much lingering on the conventional magic of name and phrase. This, at least, is the surface impression of the texture, under which some biting relevance wittily plays. First, there is the mischievous pun on Satan's having voyaged beyond the Cape of Hope. The remote and inaccessible joys of Mozambique and Saba and Arabia Felix (Englished "the blest") are carried by winds from the east; Satan, we remember, has approached Paradise from the west, so the "gentle gales" are also from the east. The voyagers *slack* their course with *such* delay; Satan has lost the impetus of his joyless speed and slackened in the duty he invented and accepted; when we return to him directly again it is to note that he has been journeying on "pensive and slow."

The further digression on Asmodeus, besides the deliberate incongruity of the fishy perfume and the anticipatory suggestion of Satan's potential love for Eve, provides an ironic contrast in tempo: "From Media post to Egypt, there fast bound." (The irony of "fast bound" is more than verbal: it looks at Satan's present lingering pace, at the driving external compulsion that Satan and Asmodeus finally share, like final fast imprisonment, and at Satan's punning bound over all bound into the Garden.) Back of the sensuous delay, the slackening course, is the great drive that carries through hell and chaos.

Satan has been identified with the sea and voyaging before — he was leviathan to the small skiff; his spear, though used as cane, made the mast of some great admiral seem like a wand; and he emerges from chaos,

> And like a weather-beaten Vessel holds
> Gladly the Port, though Shrouds and Tackle torn.
> (II, 1043f)

But the most telling echo of Satan as sea-voyager is the metaphor that links him with the merchant fleet transporting

> Thir spicie Drugs: they on the trading Flood
> Through the wide *Ethiopian* to the Cape
> Ply stemming nightly toward the Pole.   (II, 640ff)

This is, to set aside the implications of Satan as drug-merchant, the undeviating headway against the currents that we have come to expect from Satan. He has been so thoroughly businesslike before, even among the mythic variations of the archetypal Garden:

> Or other Worlds they seemd, or happy Iles,
> Like those *Hesperian* Gardens fam'd of old,
> Fortunate Fields, and Groves and flourie Vales,
> Thrice happy Iles, but who dwelt happy there
> He stayd not to enquire.   (III, 567ff)

(And there ought to have been allowable room for error here, since Beelzebub had once called the destination "The happy Ile.")

So there is Satan, "entertained," held up, suspended for the moment between past and future, guest of the hospitality of smells, diverted but not amused. Perhaps it is not too much to suggest that the "grateful smell" repeats the lovely dispensation of the "gentle gales," and is pleasing-grateful to the natural order, and is pleasing to the recipient and grateful for being received; while the recipient finds the smell pleasing and so is grateful; while Satan finds the smell pleasing and so grating.

Finally Satan enters, like a wolf, or a thief. He perches "like a Cormorant" on the Tree of Life, which is the "middle Tree" and the highest in the Garden. The commentary that follows, on Satan's misusing the tree for the meanest use of "prospect," is a commentary that extends (in anticipation) to the Garden too. It emphasizes the fallen viewpoint, the loss of the misused Garden already hanging over man. Satan does not think of the virtue of that tree, or by sitting on it regain "true Life"; instead, he sits "devising Death" and uses "For prospect, what well us'd had bin the pledge / Of immortalitie." So we move from the regaining of true life, which concerns only Satan, to the pledge of immortality, which more nearly concerns Adam. The extension of the commentary, though it includes Satan, is more pertinent to his past and to the future of Adam and Eve:

> So little knows
> Any, but God alone, to value right
> The good before him, but perverts best things
> To worst abuse, or to thir meanest use.   (IV, 201ff)

(This last goes to the heart of Adam's problem with Eve.)

The view turns downward, perhaps not without some reverberations from "meanest."

> Beneath him with new wonder now he views
> To all delight of human sense expos'd
> In narrow room Natures whole wealth, yea more.
>   (IV, 205ff)

Then the choral commentary leads the view outward, in space and time: forward to Greece, then backward to the "Sons of Eden," and finally again to this moment in time and place, "And all amid them stood the Tree of Life." And then suddenly, the last detail before the direct extended description of the Garden — what has been implied in Satan's "devising Death" and in the fallen viewpoint that preceded and accompanied the entrance into Paradise:

> and next to Life
> Our Death the Tree of Knowledge grew fast by,
> Knowledge of Good bought dear by knowing ill.
>   (IV, 220ff)

As a final detail it brings into sharp focus the perspective that has been governing the introduction to Paradise. We now ought to be prepared to look at the marvels directly.

Milton's main task in presenting Paradise is to create a commanding image of the archetype, to rediscover for us our idea of Paradise — and at the same time not to sacrifice the perspective of the larger plan. The rightness of Paradise must have reality, or there can be no dramatic conflict; but that rightness must, without ever quite losing its identity, be resolvable into the larger rightness of God's plan. The problem is a smaller and preliminary version of a major problem of the whole epic. It is involved in the problem, which Milton understood profoundly, of the self before God. And so any final understanding of Paradise can be approached only through the Fall. But this is perhaps enough to define the initial terms of the conflict.

The doubleness in Milton's Paradise has been widely enough recognized, though not, I think, in a way to lead toward critical understanding. Not many readers would with Paul Elmer More see only the ideal purity of Paradise: "The true theme is Paradise itself; not Paradise lost, but the reality of that 'happy rural seat'." [1] Mr. Tillyard's view is the more prevalent one, and it offers a misleading resolution of the doubleness. It is the easy, therefore contagious, critical trick of referring all complexities in the poem to the psyche of the writer, where problems can be made to disappear by being distributed under the correct rubrics:

The actual Paradise in Book Four consciously expresses Milton's yearning for a better state of things than this world provides: all the idealism of his youth is concentrated in that amazing description. Conscious and unconscious are at one in it. . . . Only an active man can create a living picture of sedentary bliss. Similarly the poignant sweetness of Milton's descriptions of Paradise and his ardent desire for perfection have less an existence of their own than express the enormous energy of Milton's mind. . . . Pessimism . . . is implicit in the description of Paradise, which has in it the hopeless ache for the unattainable. [2]

The concept of doubleness that can lead to critical understanding is, I think, a simultaneous doubleness — in which part does not cancel part, or receive authority for its existence from the unconscious, but maintains a kind of continuous counterpoint even *in* resolution. (If this is not clear, I trust it will become so.) Before considering the direct description of Paradise I want to return to the point of view expressed earlier: that Milton's Garden represents an archetypal state that can be known only through the metaphorical creation of an image; therefore, his Garden is an image of the archetype, a symbolic image in a dramatic situation that helps create the image and protect it at once — protect it from the naive and sentimental by consciously maintaining the ultimate impossibility of the *image* of the real archetype.

The formal outlining frame is clear enough. We begin with Satan and the symbolic reference to the Tree of Knowledge; we approach the end by gradual negatives, the symbolic references to Pluto (Satan), pagan gods, and imitation paradises; and we close the view of natural paradise, to consider man and woman, with the explicit reference to the fiend who "Saw undelighted all delight." But even within the framed formal perspective there are impure intrusions from time and fable maintaining their pressure, from outside, upon the inside. Some of the fruit is called "*Hesperian* Fables true." The river that divides into four main streams flows through many "famous" realms — that is, later, after the Fall: "whereof here needs no account." This last, which sounds like a piece of innocent literary garrulousness, makes its ironic point by a sophisticated literalness — there *is* no need to *account* for those famous realms here, because they don't exist yet, not until the story of Paradise is over, and any relationship between their fame and this blessed state must be an ironic one that certainly does not belong in any sincere description of Paradise; and so it is to be passed by, with the slightest possible trace of embarrassment, while art endeavors to tell, what is difficult enough, how things are in the blessed original state.

So far the irony has been emphasized, no doubt overemphasized, by isolating it in the context. That is to be regarded as no more than a useful preliminary step, recognition of the formal frame and some of its relationship to the central image. Let us now consider the image of the archetype. What we are faced with, to anticipate the discussion, are two intervolved images of the archetype, images created in terms of the marvelous. The first image emphasizes the rightness of the marvelous order, the second its richness, its authorized excess.

> Southward through *Eden* went a River large,
> Nor chang'd his course, but through the shaggie hill

Pass'd underneath ingulft, for God had thrown
That Mountain as his Garden mould high rais'd
Upon the rapid current, which through veins
Of porous Earth with kindly thirst up drawn,
Rose a fresh Fountain, and with many a rill
Waterd the Garden; thence united fell
Down the steep glade, and met the neather Flood,
Which from his darksom passage now appeers,
And now divided into four main Streams,
Runs divers, wandring many a famous Realme
And Country whereof here needs no account,
But rather to tell how, if Art could tell,
How from that Saphire Fount the crisped Brooks,
Rowling on Orient Pearl and sands of Gold,
With mazie error under pendant shades
Ran Nectar, visiting each plant, and fed
Flours worthy of Paradise which not nice Art
In Beds and curious Knots, but Nature boon
Powrd forth profuse on Hill and Dale and Plaine
Both where the morning Sun first warmly smote
The open field, and where the unpierc't shade
Imbround the noontide Bowrs.   (IV, 223ff)

First the rightness of the order, the authentic marvel. The pattern is one of cosmic order, of great variety fulfilling itself as a greater harmony. On a limited scale, befitting the terrestrial paradise, it is like that mystical dance in heaven:

mazes intricate,
Eccentric, intervolv'd, yet regular
Then most, when most irregular they seem.   (V, 622ff)

First there is the elemental harmony of water and sky, the divided waters of biblical cosmogony. A passage from the Creation is the best commentary on the course of the underground stream in Paradise:

Again, God said, let ther be Firmament
Amid the Waters, and let it divide
The Waters from the Waters: and God made
The Firmament, expanse of liquid, pure,
Transparent, Elemental Air, diffus'd

64

error is introduced into man's world and comes to signify wrong wandering. Back of the phrase are the echoes from hell, Belial's precious thoughts that wander, and the debates of the philosophical angels "in wandring mazes lost."

Now to consider the second image of the archetype, the richness and authorized excess of its marvelous order. This image is less "pure"; it requires our consciousness in a way that the first image does not; it is, one might say, a sustained literary metaphor, and we are supposed to know this. The first image, though a metaphor of the archetype, is not what Sir Thomas Browne would call an "easy" metaphor; its relationship with *this* world of experience is submerged in the perception of a further reality. It is a mystery, an *o altitudo* in which one ought to lose oneself: the perception is more nearly a direct sense of the primal order and rightness than an indirect sense of relationship. As the metaphor, which is the conveyance, shades into reality, we forget how we got there. (The critic's laborious dissection may, I hope, tell something of what happened and how, but it cannot touch the center, and it does not affect the renewability of the miracle. To speak personally, the pattern of order in the image, and most of all what happens to the water, never fails to move me beyond any sense that there is a metaphor operating.) Art, wantoning as in its prime, seems to disappear in the positive experience realized. Perhaps one of the reasons is that there is no literary tradition back of this art.

The most discernible difference in the second image is the effect of literary tradition — the long history of pastoral poetry with its characteristic attitudes, conventions, even styles. To the degree that Milton evokes and uses that tradition his image is less "pure," and is a more self-conscious, more sophisticated marvel. Exaggeration is a standard feature of the tradition, but that means it is not naive exaggeration, for the very familiarity of the attitudes and diction makes possible an extreme delicacy of adjustment. For instance, these charming lines from Jonson's poem "To Penshurst":

> Fat aged carps that run into thy net,
> And pikes, now weary their own kind to eat,
> As loth the second draught or cast to stay,
> Officiously at first themselves betray.

Only uninitiated fools would either believe the compliment literally or reject it on the grounds of its implausibility. The compliment is sincere enough but the terms are special; for where exaggeration is the proper and expected mode of discourse the degree, the individual quality, of the wit will make its own distinctions in its own created world. Here, the preposterous violation of the order of nature is so self-complete, so ceremonially dignified in its rhythm and gesture, so officious – a properly exorbitant pun! – that, like some of Donne's dynamic exaggerations, it tries out the perspective gained by making "a little room an everywhere." It is a fishy version of Sir Philip's noble "Thy need is greater than mine" – and this graceful gesture is no doubt preposterous from the unceremonial perspective of natural man, but it is the kind of "preposterousness" necessary to man's higher nature.

Milton's pastoral deliberately works with exaggeration, expecting the reader to recognize what is traditional in the terms of the discourse. After all, his pastoral paradise *is* the archetype, and so the authority for the fictions (that he will echo) of other poets. It is a pastoral version (though "impure") of that pure Platonic "idea of the beautiful" Milton wrote feelingly about in a youthful letter to Diodati – "a certain image of supreme beauty, through all the forms and faces of things." Here, if he is to measure up to his theme (whatever the influence of his frustrated youthful hopes!) he is *required* to wanton in his art, with full confidence in the inspired excesses of imaginative sensuousness.

And so he does, with a special kind of richness unparalleled elsewhere in the poem. (The most useful stylistic touchstones, for contrast, are the extravagant style in which Pandemonium and Death's causeway are built, and the quietly measured style of natural miracle in which the Word builds the world.) There is the richness of direct extended description:

Betwixt them Lawns, or level Downs, and Flocks
Grasing the tender herb, were interpos'd,
Or palmie hilloc, or the flourie lap
Of som irriguous Valley spread her store,
Flours of all hue, and without Thorn the Rose:
Another side, umbrageous Grots and Caves
Of coole recess, o're which the mantling Vine
Layes forth her purple Grape, and gently creeps
Luxuriant; mean while murmuring waters fall
Down the slope hills, disperst, or in a Lake,
That to the fringed Bank with Myrtle crownd,
Her chrystall mirror holds, unite thir streams.
The Birds thir quire apply; aires, vernal aires,
Breathing the smell of field and grove, attune
The trembling leaves, while Universal *Pan*
Knit with the *Graces* and the *Hours* in dance
Led on th' Eternal Spring. Not that faire field . . .

                                                    (IV, 252ff)

The generalized sensuous excitement in language and rhythm
(which are made to bear a major burden) serves more than the
argument of any single or focused detail. It is a frankly "literary"
demonstration of Paradise, the expected gorgeousness of nature
wantoning. The archetypal pattern of order is still the theme,
but these are bravura variations on the theme: beginning with
the simple sensuous varieties of landscape (in which light and
darkness are only part of the varied loveliness), but touching
again the unity of waters, and moving on to the sensuous attune-
ment of sounds and smells, and ending with the great symbol of
order in apparent irregularity, the dance. The rhythm of the
whole passage is itself an extraordinary metaphor of order; it does
not wanton, but is at once sensuously exciting and controlling.
(That is a solid esthetic fact one ought not take for granted.)

There is also a richness of intensive description, the remarkable
effect of these lines on the flowers that nature

Powrd forth profuse on Hill and Dale and Plaine,
Both where the morning Sun first warmly smote
The open field . .

It is a major miracle of imaginative sensuousness, and so perhaps one had better not try to explain it. One thing is clear: Milton is here accepting his pastoral tradition and creating a model for sensuous recognition, Paradise "To all delight of human sense expos'd / In narrow room." It would be as critically unintelligent not to admire the vowels and consonants here as to grant them completely independent value. But they are too difficult to talk about, so I concern myself with the opening three words. We seem to be witnessing the miracle in action – the pouring forth is exploded outward rhythmically by the *profuse*, which springs out of the first two words, out of their important consonants, and out of the meaning. *Profuse*, which modifies and means one thing, also retains its verbal force and means *poured forth*. It is as if what was being described then happened, by a kind of imaginative fiat: the first statement *saying* what the second *does*.

That is certainly an extravagant trick with language, one that perhaps better suits the description of Paradise than of lesser gardens. Milton, cognizant of his high theme, its obligations and its privileges, uses a modified version of this trick two other times. One is mostly the rhythmic effect, the sudden immediacy of action that springs unexpectedly from a description that has been conducted at an indefinite distance. The third line of the following is example:

> Southward through *Eden* went a River large,
> Nor chang'd his course, but through the shaggie hill
> Pass'd underneath ingulft.   (IV, 223ff)

And then there is this example: "mean while murmuring waters fall / Down the slope hills, disperst." The leisurely and melodious movement of water falling is abruptly changed to the immediate crashing fall. The rhythmic effect is perhaps at the imaginative center, but Milton has also cunningly released the verbal force of *disperst*, and the original Latin meaning, which becomes a fresh metaphor when it is the oneness of water that is being dispersed. Technically the device is rather close to the one illustrated by *profuse*. So, one may add, is the way the consonants are mar-

shaled for the sudden release — the p–r–f of "Powrd forth" and
the p–r–f of "profuse," the d–s–p of "Down the slope hills" and
the d–s–p of "disperst."

One further example of "literary" demonstration is perhaps
worth noting — because of the unmistakable self-consciousness ex-
hibited. Nowhere else, I think, does Milton so indulgently imitate
physical movements by the sound of his verse as in his amused
description of the pre-lapsarian zoo:

> th' unwieldy Elephant
> To make them mirth us'd all his might, & wreathd
> His Lithe Proboscis . . .
>   others on the grass
> Coucht, and now fild with pasture gazing sat,
> Or Bedward ruminating.   (IV, 345ff)

This is program music that expresses one of the human attitudes
evoked by the pastoral theme — in which the artist's awareness of
exaggeration is functional in the art, for this art is the grown
man's conscious love for the childhood of nature in which he
once unself-consciously participated with a child's love. The
exaggeration is part of the ritual of recognizing the impossible
lovingly, and the reader must know the terms of the metaphor,
the reciprocal relationship between the artist's and the reader's
awareness of each other's awareness. Theme and tradition require
the same basic relationship in the more formal extended description, but there the formality and the stylized expression of the
ideal maintain a greater distance (and therefore greater potential
range of distinctions) between artist and reader, between nature
and idea, between metaphor and reality.

We are never allowed to rest with the beauties of the sensuous
paradise, for they, like the self-consciousness, are only a necessary
part of the whole image. There is always the pressure of time and
the larger plan. That fair field of Enna is not introduced with re-
luctant coyness, for the sake of the fine lines alone — not with
Satan watching, ready to act out the archetype of the myth. The
Garden *is* an essential fact, and if the derivative fables are true

they are so only in their original source, where (the fact of the archetypal Hesperian fruit is small but stubbornly what it is) they are also delicious. But whatever the dignity of the Garden as place, it cannot, being subject to time and about to vanish, escape some of the ridiculousness of its ideal impossibility — where bliss is enormous, and where there is no fear lest dinner cool, and where, we are reminded, there are no grooms besmeared with gold, no "starved" lover singing to his proud fair. Milton is no more committed to keeping the Garden pure of these invasions from time than Adam is, to whom the prospect of Paradise without Eve seems living "again in these wilde Woods forlorn." Place, at that point, is well on the way to coming full circle, with the outside of Paradise, our first view with Satan of the savage wilderness, preparing us for our last view of the inside,

> an Iland salt and bare,
> The haunt of Seales and Orcs, and Sea-mews clang.
> (XI, 834f)

These two, the approach from the first fall and Adam's final vision, are part of the larger (though not the largest) frame that governs our perspective of the Garden. The sophisticated intrusions from time — including the deliberate and lovely dissonance of borrowed myth, the submerged dissonance of some original myth (as the "mazie error" of the water), and the heavy crashing dissonance of satiric reference — these are, rightly considered, part of the given image and not intrusions at all. For the image, to repeat, is not the archetype. It is an impure image in motion, under the aspects of time and God's plan, of a pure motionless archetype that is practically, if not quite historically, outside of human time, or at least on an extreme brief boundary.

I should like to try out this conclusion by turning for a final time to a concrete matter of style. Our first glimpse of the Garden, still from outside, is of the trees and their fruit:

> Blossoms and Fruits at once of golden hue
> Appeerd, with gay enameld colours mixt. (IV, 148f)

The quality of the exaggeration can better be appreciated by comparison with Waller's description of the Bermudas, the "Summer Islands":

> For the kind spring, which but salutes us here,
> Inhabits there, and courts them all the year.
> Ripe fruits and blossoms on the same trees live;
> At once they promise what at once they give.

Milton, who here owes nothing to leisurely antithesis of phrase and rhythm, can be even briefer on this point. The Tree of Life stands "High eminent, blooming Ambrosial Fruit / Of vegetable Gold." Given the tradition, with the standard expectation that the order of richness will be set out in appropriate richness of style, the most astonishing thing about the exaggeration is its brevity. It is even brusque, and that, a kind of intermittent brusqueness, is one of the strangest qualities of his description of Paradise. (To suggest, without trying to explore, a musical analogy, the brusqueness is not unlike an important quality of Beethoven's style — for instance, the scherzo of Opus 106 and of 135, much of 120 and 131, the way the theme is at last cuffed around in the finale of Opus 53, and the prettiness roughed up in the substituted finale of Opus 130.)

The brusqueness in the Garden is part of the unmelting pattern, and serves as dissonant contrast to the great immediate richnesses of harmony and as an indissoluble part of the larger harmony of the whole poem. It serves the immediate harmony by testing, strengthening, even enriching, through contrast and conflict; it serves the larger esthetic and cognitive harmony by enduring as a necessary shaping part and by this minor practical function — by not allowing us (or Milton) to rest in the sensuous richness, which would be a premature and limited resolution.

We must as human beings yearn for and love the lost Paradise, but not stay romantically at our yearning for the actual irrecoverable state. Implicit in the state is its loss. The poetry must accommodate us to both the love and the loss. The place and the fact are subject to time and cannot be willed back into existence

— except as an impostor myth, a kind of self-tempting anti-archetype, of which the self-accommodating beauty of Pandemonium is example. The pure archetype, unlike its impure image, remains unchanged, and is the source of significance and authority in its reborn image, the Paradise within, happier far.

THE FALL

THE angels fall by their "own suggestion" and "self-tempted." Man falls "deceived" by Satan. This must mean, what Milton never tries to make dramatically real, that Satan is only the spokesman of the consciousness of his followers — an internal agent rather than an external agent. The temptation must have been a kind of spontaneous mass contagion — their "own suggestion." In hell and in Paradise Satan does not maintain the relationship toward his followers that God in His omniscience has revealed. But then Satan, under conscious guilt, has partly separated himself from himself. He assumes the role of external guilty agent who tempted the part of himself represented by his followers; and being incapable of repentance, he must play out the tangled game of separate selves; his responsibility toward them will furnish him with the external moral sanction he needs in order to act, though he will then be dependent upon their dependence upon him. But Satan's followers are quite minor characters in the drama and Milton is not much concerned, it seems, with their original motivation. For Satan the fact remains: he fell self-tempted, himself (and his followers and Sin) the inner agent, with no external agent.

Adam falls deceived by an external agent, Satan. But there is an inner agent, too, for Adam is tempted by Eve and Eve is part of himself; in these terms Adam also is self-tempted — with the necessary addition, both dramatic and theological, that there is an external agent who presses home the self-temptation. It is a classic

75

form of human drama. For example: the noble Macbeth succumbing to his inner depravity pressed home externally by Lady Macbeth (who is both internal and external); and this triangle succeeded by that of the guilty Macbeth succumbing to his inner nobility pressed home externally by Macduff, who is the creature of Macbeth's conscience.

If the motives and drama of Milton's version of Adam's fall are to be as profound as they are far-reaching in significance, then the essential conflict must be internal — so that the responsibility (in human terms, which do not contradict but interpret, humanly, the divine terms) may also be internal. That is a necessary premise of the drama and paradox of Christian freedom, as Milton understands that concept.

Milton's treatment of evil seems to imply a kind of deterministic inevitability. That is partly due to the permissive privileges and the consequences of free will, which evil also enjoys. Besides, God's providence "finds its exercise . . . also in impelling sinners to the commission of sin, in hardening their hearts, and in blinding their understandings." [1] Satan is "free" to fail, as he is free to fall ten thousand fathoms through chaos, rescued only by the "ill chance" of a natural cause. But his perverse will makes the natural utmost of his chances:

With head, hands, wings, or feet pursues his way,
And swims or sinks, or wades, or creeps, or flyes.   (II, 949f)

Satan's will, which is powerfully impelled and hardened by God's providence, is characterized by excess. "Sin," as Milton writes, "is not in a predicament to be measur'd and modify'd, but is alwaies an excesse . . . and is as boundlesse as that vacuity beyond the world." [2] So Satan, moving with the power that is possible in excess, enters the Garden: "At one slight bound high overleap'd all bound." The images that accompany Satan's entrance bear out the dominant impression of the relentless drive. The prowling wolf urged by hunger easily leaps the fence that pens the flocks "amid the field secure." The thief easily gets past the burglar-proof doors — through a window. But the images in-

of
Rajan &
Tillyard

76

troduce a new argument, which has been implicit in God's grant-
ing of free will to evil as well as to good. If evil cannot be kept
out by *man's* providence, if this is how external contrivance keeps
the flocks and the cash "secure," then evil does enjoy a kind of
inevitability. Yet the inevitability of evil is an external inevitability, for the entrance of evil is in effect external, counting for
nothing by itself. The sheep and the cash are no more than annoy-
ing losses to the owners, and no more than petty spoils, physical
subsistence as it were, to evil. Only by internal victory, over the
will, can evil make the loss and the spoils major.

So entrance is easy, and perhaps inevitable, into God's Garden
(once evil has arrived there) and into God's Church (following
the consequences of the Fall); for there is no sanctity in place as
place, but only in the paradise within: which is free of evil not by
exclusion but by internal victory over the evil which is present.
Adam's comment on Eve's dream goes to the heart of the matter:

> Evil into the mind of God [3] or Man
> May come and go, so unapprov'd, and leave
> No spot or blame behind.   (V, 117ff)

And *Paradise Regained* is a great dramatic demonstration of Milton's comprehensive and solid acceptance of the role of evil.

So the defeat of Adam, if it is to be morally significant, must be
an internal defeat — a self-temptation that is pressed home externally by the cooperating self. Adam understands the formal terms
of the conflict. With tragic irony he says to Eve, before he accepts
her whim of divided labor:

> within himself
> The danger lies, yet lies within his power.   (IX, 348f)

He understands the formal terms, but the circumstances of that
danger and that power are more complex than Adam — as a whole
united being, spirit and flesh — understands, or chooses to understand. For the danger within is the Eve within himself. She, as
part of Adam, is Milton's formal internal agent.

God's Word to Adam names Eve "thy other self." It is not a
simple statement, for there are weighty implications in Eve's also

being "Thy likeness, thy fit help," and perhaps most important, "Thy wish, exactly to thy heart's desire." Adam's first reported reply is in physical terms: "Bone of my Bone, Flesh of my Flesh, my Self / Before me." Adam understands more, with his mind, but the physical nature of his first response exerts a powerful pull. Eve is, in Milton's comment on Genesis, God's gift of "another self, a second self, a very self it self." Milton's further comment is that Adam understood God's intention, and "had the gift to discern perfectly, that which concern'd him . . . and to apprehend at first sight the true fitness of that consort which God provided him." Adam might have said (interpreted, it is "as if he had said"), "This is she who was made my image, ev'n as I the Image of God, not so much in body, as in unity of mind and heart." He might have said that, yet "*Adam* spake like *Adam* the words of flesh and bones, the shell and rinde of matrimony; but God spake like God, of love and solace, and meet help, the soul both of *Adams* words and of matrimony." [4]

In exploring Adam's relations with his "very self it self" we must begin by accepting the unequivocal approval of Eve, God's explicit statement, "It is not good that man should be alone." Eve *is* part of man's given nature, right and reasonable and blessed by God. But still she is a concession to the limitations, the necessary imperfection of human nature. For man is not God, perfect in Himself, reflected in the universe but not needing that reflection, absolute in unity, not needing to "generate" or to "converse," though pleased to "emanate." Man, though as nearly perfect as a human creature could be, requires completion.

Eve must be accepted so, in the double sense of being a concession but blessed; and therefore Milton cannot admit a Platonizing concept, like Philo's, of man's original solitary perfection. Nor can Milton accept a Platonizing concept of original bisexuality; he holds to the literal distinction in Genesis: "in the image of God created he him; male and female created he them." Man is created in the image of God and woman in the image of man — "however the Jewes fable and please themselvs with the accidentall concurrence of *Plato's* wit, as if man at first had bin created Hermaphrodite." [5] Nor can Milton accept, in any literal way, hetero-sexuality as either the result of the Fall or the implied cause. For instance, Gregory of Nyssa's Hellenistic importation into the biblical concept of evil:

But as He perceived in our created nature the bias towards evil, and the fact that after its voluntary fall from equality with the angels it would acquire a fellowship with the lower nature, He mingled, for this reason, with His own image an element of the irrational. . . . it is not allowable to ascribe the first beginnings of our constitutional liability to passion to that human nature which was fashioned in the Divine likeness; but as brute life first entered the world, and man, for the reason already mentioned, took some-thing of their nature (I mean the mode of generation), he accord-ingly took at the same time a share of the other attributes contemplated in that nature. [6]

The implications of this diverge irreconcilably from the plain import of its not being good that man should be alone. But parts of the concepts of the "irrational" and the need of "fellowship" — not in any literal and approved way — are related to Milton's view of the basis of drama in man's imperfection and freedom. And the potential conflict of passion and reason is part of Milton's plan — though Milton does not accept a strict dualism, which would have Eve literally female passion (external) and Adam masculine reason (internal). That would make for too limited and superficial a conflict. While not building exclusively on any Platonizing concepts that tend to transfer the conflict and the responsibility from *within* Adam, Milton does evolve his argu-ment from ideas that owe something to Plato. Original man may not have been hermaphrodite, but Milton needs the suggested relation between likeness and love which is presented whimsically in the *Symposium*, and yet is a part of Plato's master-concept of "sameness." It offers a way of dramatizing the woman who is man's image, his other self and very self, who completes the image of God that requires "unity of mind and heart." Philo's interpre-tation, which Milton would regard as wrong, is wrong in a way that Milton can use, for it develops the risk of temptation implicit in the image of self:

79

For, as long as he was single, he resembled, as to his creation, both the world and God; and he represented in his soul the characteristics of the nature of each, I do not mean all of them, but such as a mortal constitution was capable of admitting. But when woman also was created, man perceiving a closely connected figure and a kindred formation to his own, rejoiced at the sight, and approached her and embraced her. And she, in like manner, beholding a creature greatly resembling herself, rejoiced also, and addressed him in reply with due modesty. And love being engendered, and, as it were, uniting two separate portions of one animal into one body, adapted them to each other, implanting in each of them a desire of connection with the other with a view to the generation of a being similar to themselves. And this desire caused likewise pleasure to their bodies. . . .[7]

Milton's treatment of the problem of "likeness" is much more profound than Philo's. It is at once intellectually more adventurous and theologically more sober and reasoned. But in his direct interpretations of biblical metaphor Milton tries to confine himself to a careful respectfulness — as in his comment on Genesis 1 : 26: "And God said, Let us make man in our image, after our likeness." In the cooler element of prose, this is "as if to intimate the superior importance of the work, the Deity speaks like to a man deliberating." [8] (Philo's "reasonable conjecture" is that God providently shares the creation of man with some assistants, and these may consequently bear the responsibility for what is evil in man's nature.)

In the poetic creation of Eve Milton applies and expands the simple sense of "the Deity speaks like to a man deliberating." That hint seems behind the scene in which the Deity leads Adam to define the companionship he wants. The scene is gently comic, the tone that of amused and mildly teasing benevolence, a kind of lofty pastoral dialogue between a bright, serious, young mind and timeless Omniscience kindly spelling things out. The tone doubtless reflects the general atmosphere of Eve's creation — the last act before the Sabbath, neither masterwork nor afterthought, but a sort of pleasant postponement that borders the holiday. And yet, though the dominant tone is comic, a graceful and warm scherzo, serious things are woven in, however lightly, for the record as it were. Adam, through the exercise of reason and free will, is allowed to share in this last act of creation which so nearly concerns him. That, one may reasonably interpret, is a main point of the dialogue, and it confers both a privilege and a responsibility upon Adam. It is as if the Deity said, after man had demonstrated his high degree of self-understanding, "Let us now make woman in your image."

Though the gift was intended anyway, the terms are now unmistakable. Eve cannot now be merely the part of Adam's essential nature that is creature in the natural order and subject to natural law; she must now also be part of his essential nature that includes the freedom of his spirit and corresponds to one of the three theological virtues, love. It is a mark of man's dignity that God helps him exercise his consciousness until his concept of Eve is worthy of his higher nature: "Expressing well the spirit within thee free." That which, being man, he has not been able to express God will create: "Thy wish, exactly to thy heart's desire." Though this will be gift, uniting and fulfilling the mind's and the heart's desire, it is a gift God seems to consider that Adam has at least partly earned; and Adam is allowed to participate further in the creation of Eve through the agency of his "internal sight," which witnesses the act itself.

Milton does not, like some theologians, tend to sentimentalize man's perfection before the Fall. But being strongly committed to man's undestroyed dignity ("For nothing now-adayes is more degenerately forgott'n, then the true dignity of man"[9]), he must establish that dignity in Adam's brief sinless history. And as poet he must body forth a compressed myth while inventing some proper scope of action for Adam, whose first *recorded* independent act was sinful. The self-exploration that leads to the concept of Eve allows Adam to show his dignity. His exercise of reason leads to choice, which leads to action when, through the "efficiency" of God, the desire of Adam's mind and heart is brought into being. In the last part of the action Adam is a passive participant, but it does not seem unreasonable to say that the creation of Eve constitutes a kind of responsible action for Adam.

The account to Raphael records a reaction also. In the less re-stricted element of poetry biblical metaphor can be adapted to suggest a bold argument:

> And in her looks, which from that time infus'd
> Sweetness into my heart, unfelt before,
> And into all things from her Aire inspir'd
> The spirit of love and amorous delight.   (VIII, 474ff)

The central image around which Adam expresses himself seems to reflect Adam's own creation, when God "breathed into his nostrils the breath of life." Surely Milton had speculated too much on Genesis for this image to be accidental. Adam, speaking the language of creation, greets his newly created self who in com-pleting him completes his own creation. There seems also to be suggested, on a lower plane appropriate to this secondary creation, an indivisibility of flesh and spirit — necessary and proper to "a living soul," as Milton understands the Hebraic term.

But still there is a troubling quality about this use by Adam of the image from the primary creation. Partly it is Adam's unself-conscious lending to Eve a metaphor by which God had chosen to express Himself to man's understanding — and Milton himself is acutely conscious of the nature and status of God's metaphors. Besides, the image has been significantly altered. What happens to Adam this second time is in terms of "looks," and happens through the sight, which though the noblest sense is still a sense and per-forming a function properly above its authority. The word-play on "Aire" must be thought a little dangerous; it is not less deliber-ate on Milton's part, surely, than Marvell's creative study of the word in his poem "The Fair Singer." Besides, there is another thing wrong. Adam's metaphor, though representing a mystery, is more like a kind of summary fact; a relationship, however com-plex and far-reaching, is established sensibly; and the gift is a total one, the whole gift of an inferior (not intended to measure and allot her gift) to a superior (who is intended to measure). Mil-ton's interpretation in the *Christian Doctrine* explores some of the implicit gap between God's metaphor (which emphasizes the con-cept of measure and the dramatic contingency) and Adam's:

Nor did God merely breathe that spirit into man, but molded it in each individual, and infused it throughout, enduing and embellishing it with its proper faculties . . . when God infused the breath of life into man, what man thereby received was not a portion of God's essence, or a participation of the divine nature, but that measure of the divine virtue or influence, which was commensurate to the capabilities of the recipient.   (Chapter VII)

The least that may be said is that Adam's use of the metaphor which has God's mark on it dangerously heightens things that might otherwise be considered innocent and amiable. The Eve who is part of him, whose creation he has shared in, seems – by the metaphor he grants her – to be creating him in turn, and in *her* image.

Milton must also invent some significant scope of action for Eve. We have been examining what may be considered an action, for it is perhaps not too much to say that Adam's account of her creation represents a kind of action for Eve, one that foreshadows his fall. But to look at this from another perspective, and for the moment to overlook other matters, Milton presents what turns out to be a major action in the episode of Eve's dream. First, the significant introduction to that dream. Adam wakes like an innocent child from his light airy sleep:

> And temperat vapors bland, which th' only sound
> Of leaves and fuming rills, *Aurora*'s fan,
> Lightly dispers'd, and the shrill Matin Song
> Of Birds on every bough.   (V, 5ff)

He hangs enamored over unawakened Eve,

> and beheld
> Beautie, which whether waking or asleep,
> Shot forth peculiar Graces.   (V, 13ff)

The image is more than strong, in the context of Paradise it connotes violence and anticipates the passion Adam feels for Eve, the "vehement desire," the "Commotion strange." In the ideal harmony of Paradise, where Aurora's fan disperses the bland vapors of innocent sleep, such an image is arrestingly dissonant. And though Milton's art characteristically does not pause to savor isolated surface moments of the style, yet no moment is lost in the final pattern. What shocks here is mostly the violence in Paradise of *shot forth*, but partly it is that in the ideal world the graces ought not be *peculiar*. Individuality of the real self exists in the Garden; but this kind of sophisticated awareness, and the sophisticated "literary" expression of that awareness, seems rather to belong to the natural world after the Garden. The dissonance intrudes from the conflict preparing under the surface and finding for the internal relationship of Eve in Adam the external agent in Satan who, though certainly not responsible for the violent image, *is* responsible for the glowing cheek and discomposed tresses that betoken the unquiet sleep of Eve's dream. The dissonance links Eve's passion, cultivated by Satan, her violating excursion into the peculiar graces of self-love, with Adam's passion — what is implied in the fact that *this* image is an object of his cognizance.

In a sense the image violates Paradise and is an intrusion from time that puts the pressure of history on the place. The distance between this beauty and this love and the love poetry of the fallen world seems about to disappear. The image occurs again as a strong reminder when Eve leaves Adam and Raphael to the conversation that will reach its climax on the subject of Eve and her beauty:

> A pomp of winning Graces waited still,
> And from about her shot Darts of desire
> Into all Eyes to wish her still in sight.   (VIII, 61ff)

Adam, as he displays more than he is aware the danger of his state to Raphael, remarks on his weakness "Against the charm of Beauties powerful glance." These repeated images echo, with some characteristically human development, Adam's borrowed metaphor to describe his reaction to the newly created Eve — the looks that infuse and the air that inspires.

Now to consider the dream itself. Why does Eve think the "gentle voice" is Adam's? It is not that he is the only possibility, for there are the angels "By us oft seen." Is it weakness, a potential perversion of the will, or merely ignorance and an insensitivity to style? Stylistically the voice could not be Adam's, which has already been distinguished from Eve's by a relative stiffness; even at the beginning of the interview with Raphael Adam speaks with a certain dignified awkwardness that later changes in perceptible ways. Milton has prepared a careful distinction that is here dramatically relevant, even crucial.

Some of the lovely pastoral poetry of Book IV turns out to have had this cognitive purpose, which we may examine by looking at the section that celebrates the approach of evening and the preparation for sleep. First there is the pastoral description by the narrative voice of the poem:

> Now came still Eevning on, and Twilight gray
> Had in her sober Liverie all things clad;
> Silence accompanied, for Beast and Bird,
> They to thir grassie Couch, these to thir Nests
> Were slunk, all but the wakeful Nightingale;
> She all night long her amorous descant sung;
> Silence was pleas'd: now glow'd the Firmament
> With living Saphirs: *Hesperus* that led
> The starrie Host, rode brightest, till the Moon
> Rising in clouded Majestie at length
> Apparent Queen unvaild her peerless light,
> And o're the dark her Silver Mantle threw. (IV, 598ff)

There is unmistakable love expressed for the beauty of nature, but it is a calm and unromantic love, with no nervous quiver in the sensuousness; the beauty celebrated is firmly founded on order, here on the order of day and the order of rest. Adam's twilight recital, which follows, while not altogether unsensuous, dwells almost entirely on the beauty of the natural order as symbol for the human order:

> Fair Consort, th' hour
> Of night, and all things now retir'd to rest
> Mind us of like repose, since God hath set
> Labour and rest, as day and night to men
> Successive, and the timely dew of sleep
> Now falling with soft slumbrous weight inclines
> Our eye-lids. (IV, 610ff)

The order of repose is a mark of man's dignity, for he labors in God's eye; the conclusion is practical: "Mean while, as Nature wills, Night bids us rest." What he bids, Eve "with perfet beauty adornd" obeys unargued, accepting God's law from him. She presents her own praise of the order of nature; it is a prettier poem than Adam's, more graceful and more sensuous, turning in lovely circle about Adam, who is the center giving the order its value:

> With thee conversing I forget all time,
> All seasons and thir change, all please alike.
> Sweet is the breath of morn, her rising sweet,
> With charm of earliest Birds; pleasant the Sun
> When first on this delightful Land he spreads
> His orient Beams, on herb, tree, fruit, and flour,
> Glistring with dew; fragrant the fertil earth
> After soft showers; and sweet the coming on
> Of grateful Eevning milde, then silent Night
> With this her solemn Bird and this fair Moon,
> And these the Gemms of Heav'n, her starrie train:
> But neither breath of Morn when she ascends
> With charm of earliest Birds, nor rising Sun
> On this delightful land, nor herb, fruit, floure,
> Glistring with dew, nor fragrance after showers,
> Nor grateful Eevning mild, nor silent Night,
> With this her solemn Bird, nor walk by Moon,
> Or glittering Starr-light without thee is sweet.
>
> (IV, 639ff)

Then she breaks off with a strangely dissonant abruptness:

> But wherfore all night long shine these, for whom
> This glorious sight, when sleep hath shut all eyes?
>
> (IV, 657f)

Adam lectures on order again, on the relationship between created and Creator. Man is not *the* center. His verse rises in pitch to praise, not the things, but their relationship to the Creator. Then they approach the described natural beauty of their "blissful Bower"; negative comparisons from myth ("though but feignd") and time apply their pressure to the moment, chief among them the lovely sad anticipation of Pandora. Finally they make their nocturnal devotions in praise of the Creator of nature.

The voice that Eve heard, of which she says, "I rose as at thy call," could not be Adam's. It is her voice — assumed, projected, and heightened by the tempter who is external, but who cannot effectively tempt except internally. The modest excitement of rhythm and verbal sensuousness in Eve's praise to Adam of the order of nature becomes here a celebration of the secret man-hidden parts of nature. What was potential in the earlier passage, and strongly intimated by her abrupt and curious question, here becomes explicit — an answer that emerges in distorting preoccupation, that breaks the order and the place of self in that order.

> now is the pleasant time,
> The cool, the silent, save where silence yields
> To the night-warbling Bird, that now awake
> Tunes sweetest his love-labor'd song; now reignes
> Full Orb'd the Moon, and with more pleasing light
> Shadowie sets off the face of things; in vain,
> If none regard; Heav'n wakes with all his eyes,
> Whom to behold but thee, Natures desire,
> In whose sight all things joy, with ravishment
> Attracted by thy beauty still to gaze.   (V, 38ff)

In this invitation to the "walk by Moon" the solemn bird of night now sings a "love-labor'd song" — as in the poetry of the fallen world. The light of the moon is now beautiful in a sophisticated way, setting off the face of things by shadow — a notion more proper to a world where good is known by evil. It is related to the illusion that Mr. Eliot, also working from a concept of time-less order, in "Burnt Norton" ascribes to daylight:

> Investing form with lucid stillness
> Turning shadow into transient beauty
> With slow rotation suggesting permanence.

The answer to the charming variety of moonlight is in the hymn of the next morning: "let your ceaseless change / Varie to our great Maker still new praise." But all of this is no more than the alluring threshold of temptation, the initial titillating satisfaction of sense that vaguely promises what the will perverting itself really wants. The answer to Eve's abrupt question about the beauty of night comes in the guise of an answer (an answer to the question planted in the syntax — "Whom to behold but thee"); it is an invitation to self-love presented more palatably as if from outside the self, in a voice she thinks is Adam's.

There are two other echoes worth noting, for the voice does not rest everything on the major temptation of self-love. Eve's unargued obedience to Adam's law, "to know no more / Is womans happiest knowledge and her praise," receives this cunning variation from the tempter offering fruit from the Tree of Knowledge:

> Here, happie Creature, fair Angelic *Eve*,
> Partake thou also; happie though thou art,
> Happier thou mayst be, worthier canst not be.
>
> (V, 74ff)

And then a further stage of knowledge as a means of happy self-love:

> Ascend to Heav'n, by merit thine, and see
> What life the Gods live there, and such live thou.   (V, 8of)

Here, at the climax of temptation, the flattery of merit and elevated participation is shrewdly subordinated to the major appeal, the reverberating evocative whisper that tickles her curiosity. It is a variation on the answer already produced by Eve's abrupt asking whom the stars shine for — a variation that comes like an echo, though now not the major reply of self-love to the question, but the minor insinuating reply to the feelings that prompted the question. One might describe the feelings as those of the enthusiastic immature imagination, interestingly like the extravagant expression in Milton's early verses, "At a Vacation Exercise":

> and at Heav'ns dore
> Look in, and see each blissful Deitie.

But in the formal drama of temptation these feelings cannot be a little holiday tour of the imagination. They represent a will already in the state of partial perversion, ready to dabble in self-love through pride in knowledge. Though the knowledge is that of the lowest level, most resembling vulgar prying curiosity, that does not lessen the pull of the temptation or exempt the creature from the logic of sin. If it is not a big direct plunge to embrace the pool of self-love, it is a shy small step into the powerful current. Though it is a petty allurement and not very complimentary to Eve's intelligence, the tempter seems to know what he is doing.

"Nothing now adayes is more degenerately forgott'n, then the true dignity of man." What Milton clearly means is that the degeneration is not so much in actual dignity as in the *forgetting* of true dignity. That dignity, which Adam with deliberate ignorance "forgets," is founded firmly on a concept of order. When Adam wonders about the favored place of earth and man in the universe — "How Nature wise and frugal could commit / Such disproportions" — he is, while not forgetting the basis of man's dignity, nevertheless raising a crucial question for which there is a right answer and a wrong answer. Part of Adam's first response after being created expresses a version of the right answer without raising the question at all — "And feel that I am happier then I know." That is an intuitive answer, but Adam's reason is also required to be discursive and self-conscious. The right answer requires man to recognize himself as "the Master work" of Creation, as creature with "Sanctitie of Reason" governing lower creatures:

> self-knowing, and from thence
> Magnanimous to correspond with Heav'n,
> But grateful to acknowledge whence his good
> Descends. (VII, 510ff)

Self-knowledge is based upon God's established order, upon man's knowing his proper place in that order and accepting the responsibility of his relationship upward and downward. Nature's "disproportions" properly understood lead to magnanimity and gratitude. But there is another direction possible for the mind to take, the crucial wrong answer, if Adam loses control of the idea of order. Then he will be made insecure by disproportionate appearances, will forget his true worth and consequently its basis, will be unable to maintain the balance between magnanimity and gratitude; then he will forget his true dignity and be driven to embrace disproportions above and below his proper place.

Adam's praise of nature, as we have seen, and the morning hymn to exorcise the evil of the dream, are based firmly on the idea of order. Raphael's lecture on the scale of creation is a formal explication of that order; even Satan, as an unfriendly witness, is made to contribute some unwilling though objective testimony. In speculating on the beauty of earth he perceives that the "bright officious Lamps" of heaven concenter on earth, "for thee alone, as seems." Earth, he says, like God is in the center extending to all and receiving from all:

> in thee,
> Not in themselves, all thir known vertue appeers
> Productive in Herb, Plant, and nobler birth
> Of Creatures animate with gradual life
> Of Growth, Sense, Reason, all summ'd up in Man.
>
> (IX, 109ff)

After one has discounted some of the extravagance of comparing the world to God, one is still left with a reliable image of order. Raphael, in answering Adam's question about nature's apparent disproportions, presents an authorized view that is very much like Satan's though it goes further. Excellence is not to be inferred from size or brightness, he says, anticipating the problem of Eve's beauty. The sun is itself barren, "Whose vertue on it self workes no effect"; the vigor of the sun is realized only by its effect on "fruitful Earth." And yet the bright luminaries are not "officious" to earth but to man.

Besides these and other formal statements and demonstrations of order, there are many, many images that build and extend the idea until it becomes an absolute premise of the drama. It is really more than a premise — it is a kind of sure center of unmoved right in the middle of conflict: unmoved while there is no *act* of deviation to violate the self that is part of the order, and so change that order, which must then be newly established under grace. Before we ever see Adam and Eve in the Garden the images reflect the natural harmony of the blessed state. Light and darkness are equally right, water flows above ground and under ground, and nourishes the plants that grow in shade and those that grow in light. Water is drawn upward "With kindly thirst" – for light and for its *kind*, the water above the firmament; for its enjoyed office of beneficence in the natural order, to nourish growing things that are blessedly in the center thirsting downward for darkness and water, thirsting upward for light and water. Water wanders about in the Garden with "mazie error" – before mazes become a symbol for the lost courses of human thought, and error acquires its sophisticated meaning. The medium of air plays its part: gentle gales dispense *grateful* smells, "Breathing the smell of field and grove." And the fateful morning in Paradise begins thus:

> Now whenas sacred Light began to dawne
> In *Eden* on the humid Flours, that breathd
> Thir morning Incense, when all things that breath,
> From th' Earths great Altar send up silent praise
> To the Creator, and his Nostrils fill
> With gratefull Smell, forth came the human pair
> And joynd thir vocal Worship to the Quire
> Of Creatures wanting voice, that done, partake
> The season, prime for sweetest Sents and Aires.
>
> (IX, 192ff)

The contemplation of this image of order, as Adam says in recording the lesson he learns from Raphael, is worship: the steps whereby "we may ascend to God."

Eve's retiring from the conversation between Adam and Raphael is more than expert management of the stage. Her departure makes it possible to talk about her, but more than that, she leaves under circumstances that emphasize (and create the opportunity for emphasizing) at once her genuine charms, her potentially dangerous charms (the "darts of desire"), and her relations (according to the scale of creation) with Adam. All of this must be considered her true and intended nature – even what is potentially dangerous. She is no less lovingly and sufficiently created than other of God's works. But Adam, who soundly lectures Eve on the order of nature and has his own self-knowledge reinforced by Raphael's lecture, still remains intellectually susceptible to confusion by one of nature's apparent "disproportions." When he says of Eve,

> so absolute she seems
> And in her self compleat   (VIII, 547f)

he is embracing a disproportion under the ambiguity of *seems*, contradicting self-knowledge, and violating in thought if not yet in act the idea of order. In Milton's view of human nature only evil, the self deprived of goodness and cut off from established order, can approximate absolute completeness. The conditions are special as the Elder Brother describes them in *Comus*:

> But evil on it self shall back recoyl,
> And mix no more with goodness, when at last
> Gather'd like scum, and setl'd to it self
> It shall be in eternal restless change
> Self-fed, and self-consum'd.   (592ff)

Satan comes closest to realizing that concept of the circle of self, and the serpent is very conveniently arranged in symbolic shape when Satan finally enters: "In Labyrinth of many a round self-rowld."

We must return to Adam's frank revelation of his feelings toward Eve. But what about Eve herself? To put aside her influence on Adam for the moment, she is herself involved in three preliminary gestures that tend to violate order. Her first recorded act is one that flirts with self-love — her looking into the mirror of the pool that is "Pure as th' expanse of Heav'n . . . that to me seemd another Skie." (That detail, though here still innocent, is no less charged with significance, though still potential, than the indoor lighting of Pandemonium — "as from a Sky.") There she sees, like Narcissus, the shape that both pleases and is pleased "with answering looks / Of sympathie and love." (Her first effect on herself is not unlike her creating effect on Adam — the looks that infuse sweetness and inspire the spirit of love.) And after she is led to the unshadowy author of her image she at first turns back to the watery image, for she finds him "Less winning soft, less amiablie milde."

It is all perfectly natural and innocent from our human perspective: which I suppose means that it is psychologically right — the beautiful woman opening her eyes to look into the mirror that happens to be there. And there is no more stigma attached to the act than to the evil experienced in the dream, if "unapproved." For the consciousness of Eve is not yet fully awake, and so she has perhaps not yet become a creature capable of moral responsibility. If the flaw is hinted at this does not nevertheless make it necessary; it is a flaw permitted under God's providence, but to be realized as ruinous fulfillment only through the approval, however confused and blinded, of the free will. Dramatically it is just right, pointing the possibility without prejudicing the case.

The hint is really there for *us*, as part of the external structure of the dramatic case. Satan, though he is eavesdropping and certainly not missing any usable facts, must already know where a creature is most vulnerable: he is in such matters the most experienced creature in the universe. Anyway, we are witnesses of the first innocent gesture and so can see that it is connected to the second gesture, the dream-temptation. If I am right in saying that Eve completes Adam's creation, and that her first effect on herself is not unlike her first effect on Adam (the looks that inspire love, as from a maker to the image), then it is perhaps reasonable to see this pattern occurring in a further stage. Satan at the ear of Eve seems to be endeavoring to complete her creation — in his image, the archetype of pride. He tries to "forge" illusions, or to taint her "animal Spirits" by "inspiring" venom and so raise

> Vain hopes, vain aimes, inordinate desires
> Blown up with high conceits ingendring pride.
>
> (IV, 808f)

The dream is a wedge for separating Eve from Adam by returning her to her mirror-state. Her separation-elevation breaks, though still but in a dream not yet approved, the harmony within the world of their love. It also violates the appointed order of the scale of creation.

The third gesture is Eve's whim of efficiency, her insistence on actual separation — for the ostensible purpose of getting more work done. The act is not a simple one, but there is nothing back of it, I think, that cannot be traced to the experience of the dream, which is now beginning to be approved. Most evident is her willful assertion of independence, however sweetly; and this looks back to her isolation from him in the dream, where he quickly disappears from the scene of her glorious elevation; and it looks back further to her first state, when she separates from him because she prefers the image of herself.

Adam is accurate in his analysis of Satan's aims: to withdraw "Our fealtie from God" or to "disturb conjugal Love." Only it is the major disturbance of order through the minor, the first through the second. And Adam is no more the master of his analysis than when he expresses the formal terms of the conflict — that the danger lies within himself but within his power. His arguments against separation are completely sound, manly, and affectionately considerate of her feelings. But he never recognizes what lies back of the sudden whim of efficiency, and so he does not understand that it is more than whim, that it signifies imminent danger. He praises with husbandly flattery her lovely studying of "household good," and he says what should be understood without saying in Paradise (though some of Milton's critics have had difficulty with the unfallen concept) that the appointed work is not strictly imposed labor, and that man was made not to work but to delight, "and delight to Reason joyn'd." He might have added, to the same purpose, a point from a previous lecture — that work is a distinguishing mark of man's dignity and symbolizes God's love for him. Or he might have said, interpreting Raphael, that God (Whom to obey is love) helps His creatures perfect their will through discipline.

But these arguments do not recognize and squarely face the motive for efficiency. Eve is representing work as a value *in itself*, cut off from the appointed order. Her flimsy pretense at introducing another value, that little gets done in a day and supper comes unearned, is simply irrelevant. Her valuing of work in its external aspect — not for what it means as part of man's God-given role but for what it can do, as if for the sake of itself — is perverted symbolizing. The debate quickly, too quickly, passes from its initiating point, and Eve presents in her opportunistic arguments nothing so clearly as her restless urge to have her way. But what characterizes her first point characterizes her whole position. If the argument for efficiency is an opportunistic pretext, it nevertheless is a significant one. Eve, in valuing an external for its own sake, is really valuing it for her sake: because she has nominated the value, because it represents her wish, because she has made it the means and the end for her will, and so made it a mirror of self.

If this appears to be finespun, Eve has provided us with an open demonstration. Having eaten the fruit and broken her fealty to Adam and God, but still being creature and so having an intuitive dependence upon sanction outside herself, she must posit a new order for the one she has violated. It is not a very comprehensive order, but just enough to put a kind of patch on an obvious gap. She transfers her devotion to the Tree of Knowledge, since devotion she must have. But in elevating that external object to godhead she symbolizes perversely, and with crafty self-deception. For her real value is self, and the Tree becomes a convenient external correlative of self. Under the formal ritual of worshiping it she can freely exercise self-love. It is a return to the mirror-state, now not ignorant and innocent but approved and formally rationalized. As God is reflected in the universe, imitation godhead sees itself reflected in a natural object; in this sense nature, as in the dream, becomes a mirror of self.

After she has gorged on the fruit and thrilled to the high expectation of knowledge ("nor was God-head from her thought"), she adopts a hypnotized intellectual posture not unlike that of her first recorded act — "Thus to herself she pleasingly began":

> O Sovran, vertuous, precious of all Trees
> In Paradise, of operation blest
> To Sapience, hitherto obscur'd, infam'd,

And thy fair Fruit let hang, as to no end
Created; but henceforth my early care,
Not without Song, each Morning, and due praise
Shall tend thee, and the fertil burden ease
Of thy full branches offer'd free to all;
Till dieted by thee I grow mature
In knowledge, as the Gods who all things know.

(IX, 795ff)

This is what is to become of the morning hymn in praise of order, the ritual through which Adam and Eve reminded themselves of their true selves — the selves dynamic but fixed in that order: freely mutable, with both the danger and the power within them.

As Eve turns to seek Adam, having confirmed her resolution to make him share, she pauses for further devotion. It underlines what we have already seen:

But first low Reverence don, as to the power
That dwelt within, whose presence had infus'd
Into the plant sciential sap. (IX, 835ff)

The "as" marks a nice reservation, to remind us that if it is not the tree as tree that Eve is worshiping, neither is it unambiguously the power that created the tree. And the "infus'd," though natural enough as image, has too much particular history behind it not to remind us of an already established pattern — God's metaphor adopted and varied by Adam, Eve, and Satan.

Plotinus offers an illuminating commentary on this violation of order. The terms and some of the details are necessarily different from Milton's, but the moral vision of this great writer who is a bridge between Platonism and Christianity could not be essentially different:

What is the reason that souls become oblivious of divinity, being ignorant both of themselves and him, though their allotment is from thence, and they in short partake of God? The principle therefore of evil to them is audacity, generation, the first difference, and the wish to exercise an unrestrained freedom of the will. When, therefore, they began to be delighted with this unbounded liberty, abundantly employing the power of being moved from themselves, they ran in a direction contrary to their first course, and thus becoming most distant from their source, they were at length ignorant that they were thence derived. . . . Hence, the honour which they pay to sensible objects, and the contempt of themselves. (V, i,1)

And then the souls that forget the greatness of their origin and their "true dignity," turning their vision downward "change from the whole to the part" and revert "to an independent existence." "And then when each through her separation from the whole has lighted upon some one particular part, and has deserted everything else, and turned to and entered into that one part which is subject to the impact and influence of other things, her apostasy from the whole is accomplished." (IV, viii, 4.)

What is Adam's relationship to this pattern of self-temptation we have been following? Eve's desertion of Adam is temporary; she will revert to her dependent existence, perhaps because the soul cannot separate itself from the fatherhood of intellect, or the image from what it represents. She is impelled, for reasons more profound than she articulates, to become part of Adam's very self again — and this though the larger apostasy holds. The altered image must try to alter what it represents and so construct a new order in those terms. Adam complies with startling suddenness — not because the drama is factitious and superimposed, but because Adam's conflict has been continuously involved in Eve's.

Eve's major temptation has been self-love, however decked out as knowledge or reverenced as sciential sap. Adam falls

> Against his better knowledge, not deceav'd,
> But fondly overcome with Female charm.   (IX, 998f)

The female charm is of course not merely literal and external. Milton has too carefully prepared Eve's role, and Adam's responsibility for that role, to make such an interpretation probable. Furthermore, though Adam is not deceived, and is not like Eve actively tempted by knowledge, this does not mean that knowledge plays no part in his temptation. Adam does not fall through a freakish defection of the will; there is a defection of knowledge too, for his fondness is foolish. In Eve the self-love moves from its explicit mirror-state to its dominating state, where it is implicit in the explicit adoration of knowledge. In Adam the temptations of self-love and knowledge mostly develop in implicit ways — until the actual decision, which precedes the act itself, is determined. This development is dramatically manageable because the more complicated Adam includes the Eve who is part of his very self.

Let us begin with the question of knowledge, or rather with self-knowledge — through which Adam accepts the responsibility of his relationship upward and downward, the understood position that is the basis for magnanimity and gratitude. It is only after his demonstration of self-knowledge, we remember, that Eve is given being. Appropriately the Son's reply to Adam after the Fall rejects the excuse that Eve was a *perfect* gift, restates the concept of order and Adam's obligation to that concept — "had'st thou known thy self aright." Part of Raphael's lecture on Eve takes the same significant direction:

> weigh her with thy self;
> Then value: Oft times nothing profits more
> Then self-esteem, grounded on just and right
> Well manag'd. (VIII, 570ff)

Adam's formal knowledge is quite sufficient. But self-knowledge, it would seem, is more exacting: its possession cannot be achieved, yet no withdrawal can be made from a continuous effort at achievement. Self-knowledge requires the test of action, in which the self and knowledge are both tried, separately and in relation to each other. The self must manage its knowledge, must maintain the equilibrium, which cannot be static, between magnanimity and gratitude. Indeed, Milton's master concept of the scale of creation, with every creature free to rise (in a sense) and free to fall, is a concept that requires the action of dramatic conflict in order to test and purify values — if not the real values themselves, at least creaturely understanding and possession of those values. Adam fails to distinguish, with adequate consciousness, between his formal knowledge and his self-knowledge. And this distinction, even in the state of Paradise, would seem to be necessary. Raphael's lecture on Eve only reminds Adam of what he already knows; and so Adam, after a noble defense of his delight in Eve and of the true nature of their marriage, can still assume that since he knows what is right any revelation of his feelings is innocently irrelevant. He even sounds a little hurt, as if his frankness had been misunderstood to be frankness without knowledge:

> Yet these subject not; I to thee disclose
> What inward thence I feel, not therefore foild,
> Who meet with various objects, from the sense
> Variously representing; yet still free
> Approve the best, and follow what I approve.
>
> (VIII, 607ff)

That statement, preceding so briefly the events of the following morning and noon, cannot be a satisfactory reflection of unfallen knowledge; and yet one cannot know for sure until the event, after knowledge has been tried in action. Raphael, who knows the event, makes no effort to lecture directly on that point but contents himself with a final reminder not to let judgment be swayed by passion. Looked at from one perspective, Adam is to be presumed right until proved wrong, innocent until guilty. Theologically, and symbolically, he is innocent until he has to act. But Milton could not construct his fiction entirely from that perspective; he needed a scope of action sufficient for conflict, and he needed both direct and symbolic action that could borrow meaning, as it were, by anticipating human experience after the Fall. What Adam says here *is* innocent, though it reminds us of the innocence of Eve's unapproved dream; from the event and our consequent perspective Adam is already undergoing the conflict of temptation, and does not *know* that. He is anticipating — and that is why we can see it — the fallen self-righteousness that assumes itself virtuous because it *knows* what is right.

It is the kind of pride that Paul describes as resting in the law, the confidence of him who has "the form of knowledge and of the truth in the law." (Romans 2:17–20.) He has been a teacher of Eve but is unaware that he may not be the master of his knowledge. He is overestimating the power within himself by underestimating the danger within, and he will soon repeat that mistake toward Eve — when he lets her separate while he rests confidently in a concept of *freedom* that offers its guarantee to the human spirit only because it demands the utmost in self-consciousness. He can warn Eve accurately of the "faire appeering good," the "specious object" that may deceive reason to misinform the will — but that is a formal warning, to an independent self, of an external object that can be a danger only when it is internal and no longer recognizable formally as object.

This warning resembles the analysis already made of his own danger, where he also expects a recognizable object, the Eve who is external to him and not his very self. His easy confidence in the face of the imminent danger he does not recognize is directly parallel to Eve's blithe confidence in being able to conquer any external temptation Satan may present. In both Adam and Eve at these crucial points one may suspect a certain protective self-deception — Eve's to assert herself and to flirt with the secret temptation, Adam's to preserve the deliciousness of the inner temptation by recognizing it only externally, and so resting in his conscious mastery over what he is enjoying. To borrow Tertullian's term for fallen nature, both Adam and Eve seem to be permitting a kind of "willing ignorance" in their self-deception.

Another action, small but apparently related, seems to suggest a further parallel. Adam's unexpected question to Raphael, about sex in heaven, has a strange resemblance to Eve's irrelevant curiosity about whom the stars shine for. It is true that the answer is a dignified statement that follows from Milton's fundamental concept of the order that includes both flesh and spirit. But the dignity of the answer does not quite cover the strangeness of the question and the circumstances of the question — as Adam's dignified answer does not alter the significance of Eve's question and of the state of mind implied by her asking it. Adam's freedom of mind, it would seem, is not quite free of "idle curiosity" and "wandering thoughts"; and though he knows enough to lecture Eve, he is apparently susceptible to *approving* the same state of mind in himself — at least to the stage of articulation.

More significant, though, is the demonstrated fact that he is insufficiently impressed by his own problem with Eve; otherwise he could not with such irrelevant abruptness turn so glibly to a problem that is external to himself and diverts attention from where it ought to be concerned. Raphael's angelic blush and obliging but metaphorical answer shift the focus and the embarrassment to himself — but not, I think, entirely. We are left with a striking reminder that if Eve is part of Adam and may reflect him, he also may demonstrate, and reflect, the Eve who is part of him. And, further, self-knowledge for Adam requires his understanding the Eve who is part of himself, his very self, and not merely an external object presented "from the sense" to the judgment of the mind.

Like Eve Adam is involved in three preliminary gestures that tend to violate order; they do so in the appropriate framework of his particular responsibility: to self-knowledge, to reason itself, which is fundamental to self-knowledge, and finally to freedom. The first gesture we have already discussed in another context, Adam's account of his first response to Eve's creation — the looks that infuse and inspire, that complete his creation in the altered metaphor of the first creation, that suggest at the worst the possibility that Adam is being created in her image. That is parallel to Eve's first mirror-state of ignorant self-love, and by itself as innocent and natural as her first gesture. The self-love is only potential, in the disordering of that love through excess; but sin, we remember, "is always an excess."

The second gesture that potentially violates order, though not yet approved in act, is Adam's revelation to Raphael of his feelings toward Eve. Perhaps his most important statement — even more significant than his tentative shifting of the responsibility to nature, or his wondering admiration of passion and the "charm" of beauty's powerful glance, or his diffidence toward wisdom — is this:

> yet when I approach
> Her loveliness, so absolute she seems
> And in her self compleat. (VIII, 546ff)

Eve cannot be absolute and complete. Adam knows that as well as Satan does when he elevates Eve to absoluteness in the temptation of the dream. But Adam does not say she *is*, he says *she seems*. And he presents his whole extravagant praise of Eve deliberately as an illusion, one that he presumes to control by his formal daylight knowledge of reality. This adventure in illusion I take to be parallel to Eve's dream; in both experiences, we discover, the illusion that is enjoyed in spite of formal disapproval corrupts the control of reality. And if Eve's illusion is projected by means of an inner conflict that she must bear some responsibility for, what are we to say of Adam's conscious flirting with his daylight dream? He is entirely responsible. As Eve's dream serves to return her to the first mirror-state and to confirm that state, Adam's rationalized illusion confirms what is for him the parallel state — his response to the looks that infuse and inspire.

The third gesture is Adam's permitting Eve to work separate. Here both of them, though from different motives, unite in violating order. This is the casual decision that already sponsors the act, but each of them is too pleasantly gripped by his hidden dream to disengage himself for unpleasant recognitions. Eve by her act of separation finally approves the self-love potential in her first preference of the image of herself. The eating of the apple is as good as done. Adam, when he approves her will though against his reason, confirms the violation of order potential in his contrived illusion. Those first looks that inspired can now no longer be innocent, for *they* (and not the façade of her argument) have made Adam violate his reason and his self-knowledge, his magnanimity and gratitude, his accepted position of responsibility upward to God and downward to Eve. In place of the image of God and the spirit of life breathed into him — "that measure of the divine virtue or influence, which was commensurate to the capabilities of the recipient" — he is now preferring the sweetness infused by her looks, preferring her image to God's. They are now both united in preferring that image. The eating of the apple is for Adam only a formal act, which is nicely appropriate to his resting in formal knowledge: he is as good as fallen, and shows all of the characteristics of fallen nature before he sets teeth in the apple — when he, with a decision as spontaneous as a physical act, agrees to join her fate in violation.

Eve's violation of order is through self-love, and she expresses that by hoping to rise above her finite being through knowledge — beyond the limits she has accepted in relation to Adam: "to know no more / Is womans happiest knowledge and her praise." She forgets her true dignity and its basis in the attempt to embrace what is above her, deity. But that turns out to be no more than self-love, which requires the debased transfer of devotion to the Tree of Knowledge as a mirror of self, and requires the rationalized seduction of Adam, who must share in the violation, whether it is proved by events to be a breach upward or downward. Adam's violation — to pass for the moment the full question of self-love — is downward: through accepting unqualifiedly his finite being, by rejecting the image that through self-knowledge leads upward. He allies himself to Eve's completeness and absoluteness, accepting against reason one of nature's apparent disproportions. Knowledge does not directly tempt unfallen Adam, as it does Eve, for he is being tempted downward not upward. That does not, one might note, necessarily disqualify him from self-love. The danger within him works through his trust in himself and in his mastery over the knowledge he has. That constitutes a kind of pride and self-love, to which the key is, as for Eve, knowledge. The antithesis of the directions is resolvable in a concept of sin which would regard Eve's misguided ambition as the insecurity of an inferior seeking an impossible secure exaltation in self-love, and would regard Adam's complacency as the insecurity of a superior seeking an impossible secure debasement in self-love. Milton's archetypal situation, if we have been accurate in exploring it thus far, will already explain most of the familiar predicaments of pride that depend on and from the original sin.

Milton also assimilates into his Christian archetype certain Platonic explanations. I cannot presume to rehearse the whole relationship, for it is very complex and difficult to assess, and I am not competent. But one development seems clear to me. Part of Milton's drama is based on a mythic conflict between the soul (Eve) and the intellect (Adam). In one relationship the soul assumes the role of beauty and the intellect the role of wisdom. The mystery that befuddles the intellect is the powerful "charm" of beauty, which the confused intellect tries to understand in terms of its own high value, wisdom. Adam makes that association when he reveals to Raphael that Eve in her loveliness *seems* absolute and complete:

> so well to know
> Her own, that what she wills to do or say,
> Seems wisest, vertuousest, discreetest, best;
> All higher knowledge in her presence falls
> Degraded, Wisdom in discourse with her
> Looses discount'nanc't, and like folly shewes;
> Authoritie and Reason on her waite,
> As one intended first, not after made
> Occasionally; and to consummate all,
> Greatness of mind and nobleness thir seat
> Build in her loveliest, and create an awe
> About her.   (VIII, 548ff)

Adam, trying to explain to himself and to anticipate Raphael's objections (which he already knows), is uncomfortably attempting to rationalize a mystery that he does not quite understand — beauty that seems ascendant over intellect. What he does not face is that the mystery may be a false one, in the beholder's eye — intellect betraying itself, turning its vision downward to multiplicity instead of upward to the One, and all the while enjoying the illusion of controlling the illusion through the tricky perspective of *seems*. Raphael, with a peremptory Platonism that fits the occasion by being somewhat stricter than Milton usually allows, calls that transporting beauty an "outside." Eve states the rightness of the case more moderately, after she has recovered from her initial preference of her own image to see

> How beauty is excelld by manly grace
> And wisdom, which alone is truly fair.   (IV, 490f)

Adam receives his ironic recompense in the separation scene, where beauty acts out the mystery that Adam has tried to explain. There beauty knows her own so well that wisdom is discountenanced and approves the illusion. Eve is imperturbably sweet, and Milton builds a kind of terribly comic scene by a merciless emphasis on that quality of hers. The sweetness, however, though it may still infuse into Adam, turns deliciously inward as the secreted balm of self-pity for wounded absoluteness. Milton, though he probably did not need such, might have got a hint for the comic relation between beauty and wisdom from the wry remark by Socrates in the *Phaedrus*:

But of beauty, I repeat again that we saw her there shining in company with the celestial forms; and coming to earth we find her here too, shining in clearness through the clearest aperture of sense. For sight is the keenest of our bodily senses; though not by that is wisdom seen, for her loveliness would have been transporting if there had been a visible image of her, and this is true of the loveliness of the other ideas as well.

And for some straight intellectual distinctions one may refer to the analysis of Plotinus:

This beauty which attaches to bodies is accidental to them, for these bodily forms exist in them as in matter. . . . What then makes a body beautiful? In one sense the presence of beauty, in another sense the soul which fashions them and introduces this form into them. What then? Is the soul of itself beautiful? No, it is not. . . . So then beauty in the soul comes by wisdom. And what is it that gives wisdom to the soul? Is it not of necessity the intellect? . . . And this is beautiful of itself. Must we here make our stand as if we have arrived at the first term, or is it necessary to go beyond even intellect? Now intellect precedes the first principle in relation to us, and standing as it were in the vestibule of good, it of itself announces all things, for it is the image of that good, although it is multiple and the good remains a unity. (V, ix, 2)

In short, the soul is beautiful through its participation upward in the right order of the chain of being; the beauty of the form is "an image of real existence" that "comes from something without, refers thither, and is an image thereof." (V, ix, 5.)

The basis for the internal drama between soul and intellect lies in the concept of soul as the agent of intellect. Though the soul is the image of intellect and is the female "receptive principle" while the masculine intellect is as it were the "form," nevertheless the soul expresses the intellect — whether in direct action or symbolic action (as that of words):

In fact, just as a thought expressed in words is an image of the thought in the soul, so she (soul) is both the thought of the intellect and the entirety of its activity and the life which it sends forth to constitute a new form of being. An illustration of what I mean is fire (intellect) which has both an inherent heat, and a heat which it radiates.   (V, i, 3)

The intellect, which is like the One, also emanates a power which is "a particular form of itself." And this expression, "this activity proceeding from essence is soul." It is begotten with no change or motion in the intellect, as there was no change or motion in the principle that begot intellect and was prior to it.

But the soul does not create, abiding in her changelessness, but in change and motion she generates an image. Looking to the source of her existence, she is filled with intellect, but when she proceeds to other and opposite motions then she generates an image of herself.   (V, ii, 1)

We have gone over some of this ground in following the course of Eve's apostasy, and we must try to follow her drama a little further in these symbolic terms. But first we must look at matters again from the perspective of intellect. How, Plotinus asks, is the intellect, which may be figuratively understood as the image of the One, actually generated by the One? The answer is that what is generated turns back to behold what has generated it, and through this action is: "This vision is the intellect."   (V, i, 7.) And, further, the essence of intellect "consists in a kind of awareness of its possibilities and powers. It defines then through itself its own being by virtue of the possibilities got from the One."

Plotinus is obviously less occupied with the conflict potential in intellect than with the conflict, shrewdly analyzed, in soul. But still, if only by implication (and the fact, too obvious for Platonic discussion, that there are contemptible examples of untrue intellect), there is a basis for conflict in the responsible position of intellect between the One and soul. It would seem that even in Plotinus the vision of intellect upward does not fulfill *all* the laws of creation, for intellect must also express itself through the activity of soul. In Milton, as we have seen, self-knowledge is of crucial importance. So is the necessity of definition. (I am ignoring this difference in emphasis: whether the self knows itself mostly through knowing God, or knows God mostly through knowing self.) Self-knowledge is the vision of intellect upward, but it is firmly based on a concept of responsibility, which maintains a necessary equilibrium for the relationship of intellect with what is above it and what is below.

Milton does not disagree with Plotinus, or with St. Thomas, that the ideal contemplation of intellect is the blessed vision of God. That constitutes a kind of action — though a Puritan might regard it as more possible of practical fulfillment in Paradise. As we have seen, one action of the intellect that Adam expresses is the worship of order — the contemplated steps through which we ascend to God. But for Milton intellect must do more than contemplate God in blessedness. It must act. And though the scope of action is limited in Paradise, limited and determined by the mighty negative, action still is necessary. And action is through the soul.

Or one might say that the intellect in this drama acts by not acting; that it withdraws itself from resignation in God's will, which happens to be expressed mysteriously but unquestionably by the great prohibition, which is of course a symbolic expression not of God but of man and his nature as God in His providence knows it. In withdrawing itself the intellect allows itself to be allied passively with the active will of the soul, which is elevated to superiority by the sufferance of the intellect. This violation permits the further violation that intellect then also accepts. The evil is in the act of not acting; it is the privation of intellect from good, in an Augustinian sense; or the Platonic pure lack of form in matter. Evil that is characterized by privation is "stupidly" evil — as Satan, abstracted from his evil by the "rapine sweet" of Eve's beauty, is left "stupidly good."

That it is necessary for the intellect to act through the soul, and that some scope of proper action is possible in Paradise, Adam has demonstrated by the admirable exercise of self-knowledge that precedes and in a sense participates in the creation of Eve. A further example is the instructive worship of order that turns the soul upward from its inclination to generate an image of itself. And up to a point the intellect is still expressing itself properly in the rational argument to dissuade the soul from its urge to express itself by seeking the independence of separation. So much for the intellect which acts, or defaults, through the soul. Admittedly the drama is there mostly by implication unless we supplement Platonic terms with a biblical concept of evil.

And now finally to the soul again. Having as it were generated an image of herself in separation, Eve is nevertheless compelled to return to Adam — in order to share her new fate with him, for better or worse. Her expressed motives are mixed and confused, they are corrupted and must in turn corrupt; but there is no doubt of the sincerity in her compulsion, of the physical, and more than physical way she shows herself tied to him. The female charm of the soul that seduces the intellect to prefer beauty before wisdom still strives after wisdom. The soul practicing self-love in terms of knowledge, and generating an image of self, still strives, though perverted, after its source. For the order, though violated in fact, remains the Idea of order. And Eve's corruption is not complete. To quote Plotinus again: "What is begotten holds another and lower place than what begets, yet each thing remains identified with that which it follows, as long as it seeks after it." (V, ii, 2.) Paradoxically, if Eve had not returned to tempt Adam her apostasy from him and from the whole would have been complete. Though perverted, her act is one that affirms the moral order. And perhaps it is not irrelevant to ask whether, had she instead so denied him, she would have been redeemed through grace.

Some final questions must now be considered — these are mostly problems remaining in questions that have been partly explored. A kind of self-love has been distinguished in Adam — the trust in himself and in his knowledge, the preference of the image he has begotten to the image in which he is begotten, the withdrawing from self-transcendence upward to embrace his finite being as creature. Related to this is the question of Adam's violation of the freedom fundamental to reason and self-knowledge. And the question of self-love cannot be entirely separated from the question of love. Also, a final word must be said about Satan.

To begin with this last, let us return briefly to the external agent of the drama and to his relationship with Adam. Within the limited frame of Adam's drama there is not much direct relationship. Satan works through Eve and Adam does the rest. Yet much of the extensive treatment given Satan would be ornamental digression — which it certainly is not — if there were not some relevant larger parallels between his experience and Adam's. What happens within the limited drama, though minor, deserves at least brief mention. The scattered hints of Satan's sexual rivalry for Eve seem deliberate enough, but they are never allowed to become more than hints, a useful but small contribution to the drama. More important is Satan's reacting like Adam to Eve's beauty. When the tempter first sees Eve alone ("As one who long in populous City pent"), he reflects Adam's attitude in liking the natural beauty of Paradise better for this higher work of beauty, Eve. That, ironically, is a right view of Paradise, so long as it is contained in the larger view of order.

There is an interesting verbal parallel too: for both Satan and Adam, Eve *sums* up all delight. And Satan too is sweetly *transported* by her looks. Though there is no infusing or inspiring, he is overawed by "her every Aire." Given the situation, Eve's beauty is terrible to Satan for it bereaves him of his evil and therefore leads to good. That makes an interesting variation on the main theme of Adam's position. Besides, there is a kind of collaboration between Satan and Adam in their praise of Eve. Adam's frequent praise, though not wrong in itself or in its recognition of their relationship, nevertheless does fit into the pattern of her vanity which Satan exploits. And Adam, in his daydream of her absoluteness — the evidence of which could not have been lost on Eve — is an unwitting junior partner in tempting her with an illusory exaltation.

It is possible to go on enumerating small parallels, but the whole scope of the relationship may perhaps be understood by the bare mention of three major examples. First, the problem of love and likeness, the drama of Adam and his image, is foreshadowed by Sin's casual but important remark to Satan:

> Thy self in me thy perfect image viewing
> Becam'st enamour'd.   (II, 764f)

Secondly, both Satan and Adam fall in the name of freedom and have to work out the consequences of what they have hidden under that name. Finally, the Adam who has decided to eat the apple adopts the comic role of Satan:

>   so God shall uncreate,
> Be frustrate, do, undo, and labour loose,
> Not well conceav'd of God, who though his Power
> Creation could repeate, yet would be loath
> Us to abolish, least the Adversary
> Triumph and say; Fickle their State whom God
> Most Favors, who can please him long? Mee first
> He ruind, now Mankind; whom will he next?   (IX, 943ff)

It is trivial, as Tillyard observes, and like Eve's fatal reasoning, but it is much more than that. It is a full expression of Satan's mind, presuming to understand by reasoning from self. And we recognize at once, from the extended dramatic example of Satan, what lies ahead of Adam; as we recognize in Adam's acceptance of his guilt his refusal to play out the established role of Satan.

So far much has been made of the oneness of Adam and Eve. But it must be recognized that Milton clearly holds to a Christian concept of the uniqueness of the self. When Adam calls Eve "an individual solace dear," the words are weighed. As "there ought to be an individuality in marriage," there must be an individuality in the separate members who compose the union. In the practical affair of married living this will mean that both marriage and "charity" are less injured when each person behaves thus: "First to himself, next to whom he next owes it." To the argument that a man must love his wife as himself and therefore there can be no more separation than between body and soul, Milton replies:

I Answer: if hee love his wife as himself, hee must love her so farre as hee may preserv himself to her in a cherfull and comfortable manner, and not so as to ruin himself by anguish and sorrow, without any benefit to her . . . And that to divorce a relative and *Metaphorical* union of two bodies into one flesh, cannot be likn'd in all things to the dividing of that natural union of soul and body into one person, is apparent of it self.[10]

In working out the dramatic fiction of the first marriage Milton has to put more trust in the metaphor he has committed himself to, and follow its consequences further than in a limited prose argument. But the basis for the distinction will hold in either case. Back of this working example of pragmatic ethics is the far-reaching concept of the individual bound as individual to the will of God, and loved as individual by God. "Weigh her with thy self," Raphael advises. He is not attempting to define a whole relationship that must, since it is necessary, include some subjective and intervolved elements; but he is nevertheless, for a special situation, insisting on a certain necessary measure of separateness that is based on human requirements that go beyond the immediate situation. Proper self-esteem, he goes on to say, is grounded on "just and right," which must be *managed*, and *well*. The problem is perhaps related to the self-consciousness that must precede higher consciousness.

There is a practical way in which the distinction of individuality works in the drama. It makes definition possible, and definition is part of the dramatic concept of a writer largely concerned with temptation: "All arts acknowledge that then only we know certainly, when we can define; for definition is that which refines the pure essence of things from the circumstance."[11] Milton is much occupied throughout the poem with conflicts between *inside* and *outside* that lead to definition. Baldly stated in prose we may have something like this: Adam "might well know, if God took a rib out of his inside to form of it a double good to him, he would far sooner dis-joyn it from his outside, to prevent a treble mischief to him." [12]

In the poetry the drama is seldom a simple dualism. To mention a single example: Adam's half-abashed justification of what the angel has censured as the overvaluing of Eve's "outside." Adam replies that he is not so much delighted by her fair outside as by the demonstration of harmony between them — "in us both one Soule." But he is not subjected or foiled by what he has disclosed, "What inward thence I feel." The *inward* feelings are directly connected, in the context, to Eve's outside, her loveliness — the cause is outside, the effect inside. But Adam's true inside is in the mind "And inward Faculties, which most excell." And Raphael's parting words focus the conflict: "Perfet within, no outward aid require." But the outside is necessary to define the true inside.

Individuality, understood in its largest sense, helps define freedom and love. The Son, we remember, praises Adam's reasoned demonstration of the need for an Eve as "of thy self / Expressing well the spirit within thee free." That linking of the self with freedom, after which Eve is created, links Eve to Adam's higher nature in love and freedom. Kierkegaard's brilliant analysis of human freedom accurately describes, it seems to me, Adam's state in "choosing" Eve:

I posit the absolute and I myself am the absolute; but in complete identity with this I can say that I choose the absolute which chooses me, that I posit the absolute which posits me; for if I do not remember that this second expression is equally absolute, my category of choice is false, for the category is precisely the identity of both propositions. That which I choose I do not posit, for in case this were not already posited, I could not choose it, and yet if I do not posit it by the fact that I chose it, then I did not choose it. It exists, for in case it were not in existence I could not choose it; it does not exist, for it only comes into being by the fact that I choose it, otherwise my choice would be an illusion. . . . I choose the absolute. And what is the absolute? It is I myself in my eternal validity. . . . But what, then, is this self of mine?

If at the first instant I were to give the first expression for this, my answer is: It is the most abstract of all things, and yet at the same time it is the most concrete — it is freedom.[13]

When Adam misunderstands Eve he misunderstands himself. Both errors are in terms of freedom. "Yet still free / Approve the best," Adam says to Raphael after he has disclosed his inner feelings toward Eve. "Go; for thy stay, not free, absents thee more," Adam says to Eve in letting her separate.

In both its largest sense and in ironic variations freedom is a major theme of the epic. The Son "freely" puts off His glory, to fulfill justice through love. The infinite goodness of God, Adam tells Eve, is "As liberal and free as infinite." And it is "With liberal hand" that Eve gives Adam the fruit. She plans to take good care of the full branches "offer'd free to all," she contemplates the profit of "inward freedom" and the hazard that it may be interrupted by death, she wonders about keeping "the odds of Knowledge . . . for inferior who is free?" The central theme and the variations require us to respond to the cumulative weight now suddenly brought to bear by Adam's unexpected and casual reversal, "Go; for thy stay, not free, absents thee more." It is ostensibly an act of love, in terms of her freedom and individuality. Does it involve self-love? Absents thee more: from whom? Not from herself but from him. What is phrased as concern for her individuality, in terms of her freedom, rejects his better judgment in order to have her absent less. And is he not putting that value above her real welfare as her? — and neglecting her true and real individuality as his reason understands it? He is at the same time neglecting his own welfare — misunderstanding the danger to his individuality in this false valuing of hers, and misunderstanding the danger to his individuality in the danger he is permitting her to try. Most of all, is he not treating Eve's individuality and her freedom as values in themselves (as Eve did work and efficiency) cut off from all other respect but himself, and so values really for himself, as a mirror of self? Or put in more physical terms, is he not intent on keeping their relationship as he most enjoys it?

When the crisis comes Adam's reactions are in terms of the

"Link of Nature" — the flesh of flesh and bone of bone. Individuality and love are reduced to the limits of the flesh and bone:

> My own in thee, for what thou art is mine;
> Our State cannot be severd, we are one,
> One Flesh; to loose thee were to loose my self.
>
> (IX, 957ff)

The self that is flesh has given up freedom and individuality. Love restricted to flesh is then the only choice possible. That still represents choice, as even, to be extreme, a spasm of the flesh represents choice — though not of the reason, and still less of the "unity of mind and heart." Freedom, reason, and love, which are the human creature's endowments for ascending to God and heavenly love, are used to turn himself back on himself to embrace his creaturely temporal state as an all. Is not this choice of flesh, this expression of self, self-love? If we translated the case into other terms we should still have to admit that Adam is being selfish, and admit further that Adam is letting a short-sighted unselfishness (giving Eve her "freedom") conceal his real selfishness. A purely secular drama would have to admit this. For the theologians, of course, the case is clear and the terms classic.

To Augustine, distinguishing between the original rightness of the flesh and the consequences of sin, the flesh is good:

In its own kind and degree the flesh is good; but to desert the Creator good, and live according to the created good is not good, whether a man choose to live according to the flesh, or according to the soul, or according to the whole human nature, which is composed of flesh and soul, and which is therefore spoken of either by the name flesh alone, or by the name soul alone. For he who extols the nature of the soul as the chief good, and condemns the nature of the flesh as if it were evil, assuredly is fleshly both in his love of the soul and hatred of the flesh; for these his feelings arise from human fancy, not from divine truth.[14]

To Aquinas, relating preference for the "created good" to self-love in terms of excess: "Every sinful act proceeds from an inordinate desire for some temporal good. Now the fact that anyone desires a temporal good inordinately is due to the fact that he

loves himself inordinately." [15] From the point of view of the theological drama, the self-sacrifice of letting Eve physically absent
herself from him is a travesty of sacrificing the temporal good for
the sake of the eternal. Under the formal pattern of evil defaulting
stupidly, there is more than a suggestion that evil is playing good
and proposing inordinate desire under the guise of measured self-
discipline.

In loving Eve Adam is not really loving his very self. He is
loving *himself* as her, not loving *her* as himself. For one thing, he
is loving himself inadequately. Overconfident in himself and his
knowledge, in the obedience of his knowledge to self and of self
to God, he forgets, in centering on self, the true dignity of the
self related to God. In loving himself inadequately he cannot love
her as himself, for the love is not simply between the two of them
without extension. Adam can neither love himself adequately nor
love Eve as himself unless he can love God adequately — and so
make his love for Eve, the unity of their shared self, an expression
of that higher love.

Love is, among other things, a discipline in self-transcendence.
In angelic love, Raphael says, "Total they mix, Union of Pure
with Pure / Desiring." Angels need no "conveyance." Earthly
love, though "both the way and guide" that leads to heaven, fails
of totality — except perhaps for a false totality that restricts love
to its conveyance, the flesh. But aside from this difference, which
must be charged to the difference between man's mixed nature
and the pure spirit of higher creation, both kinds of love resemble
each other in their ritual of self-transcendence. Angels also need
intermediaries between them and God: they have the various
forms of imposed discipline to perfect the will, they have love for
each other, and they have the Son who interprets the Father. Man,
who is more imperfect, needs an intermediary too: an equal
though lesser part of himself through which he may define and
purify himself, and so rise above himself toward God. That ar-
rangement reflects man's place on the scale of creation — the dust
into which God breathed "that measure of the divine virtue or
influence, which was commensurate to the capabilities of the re-

cipient." Definition is determined by dramatic trial; rising toward God can be expressed only by myth, but false myth can be distinguished from true only by dramatic definition.

Adam's loving himself as Eve is a false myth of self-transcendence that is tested and exposed by the drama. The self that is defined is avoiding the higher responsibility of freedom to accept a debased existence founded and centered on the creaturely self. The self-love of Eve (like Satan's, though on a smaller scale) defines itself as aspiring to deity. After the Fall both sins include each other. One may consider these two sins as the extreme poles in a drama that requires action from the freedom exposed to these two contrary pulls. Each part of man's nature is attracted by what is most opposite. The Adam of knowledge descends from his true self into the creaturely self of his lower nature. The Eve who completes mind with heart transcends her true self in an ignorant search of God through knowledge. One might say, though putting it rather crudely, that the drama defines the true inside (Adam's mind) of the true outside (Adam's heart) by the false inside (heart) of the false outside (mind).

Up to the Fall the unmoved center of drama is the Idea of order, which defines the violation upward and the violation downward. Rising out of that definition is the minor myth of the soul seeking its source in intellect; ignorantly violating order downward by seeking an image of self, violating order upward by ignorantly seeking its source through intellect and beyond intellect; but still affirming the Idea of order even in the act of violation. Related is the minor myth of the attraction of opposites; intellect seeking, through the debasement of self, a falsely static freedom from the dynamic freedom of contingency; soul seeking, through the elevation of self, a falsely dynamic freedom from the true freedom of its contingency; yet both affirming in their counteractions the Idea of order. Both actions include each other; for Adam embraces Eve's aspirations, praises her "Sapience," while they both imagine they feel "Divinitie within them breeding wings"; and Eve responds to the "Carnal desire enflaming" Adam, which she "As wantonly repaid; in Lust they burne." Whatever

Heraclitus once meant by his enigmatic fragment, "The way up and the way down is one and the same," it may still serve as a formulation of these counter-adventures in violation that end the same and affirm what they violate.

Out of the tragic definition there is also a major myth which rises purified. It has the form of drama: the evil of violation is the center, belief in man's evil and belief in man's goodness are the two poles. Within that form definition continuously purifies, but what it purifies continuously passes beyond dramatic definition into the great and central mythic vision. One pole is a secure Augustinian anti-Pelagianism. The other pole is Milton's Christian Platonism (plus a Hebraic emphasis on man's wholeness, body and spirit), which affirms the dignity of man's original state, the dignity implicit in man's present potentialities (*not* wholly crippled by the Fall), his responsibility, the dignity but proper limits and directions of knowledge. In between, fully embraced, is the "logical absurdity," the paradox of original sin: the evil that looks two ways, led up to and away from; that fixes and defines man's evil (then and now), his original dignity and his present potentiality, his responsibility (then and now), the necessity and limits of knowledge, the strength and weakness, the weakness and strength of love; that makes the Fall truly fortunate by affirming the true myth of death as a condition for rebirth; that allows Adam to accept the responsibility for his evil by accepting (unlike Satan) his ultimate responsibility toward good, and so receive grace.

Before the Fall the highest value is knowledge (including self-knowledge) under which are subsumed obedience and love. Through Adam's faith in knowledge, and the irrational disobedience of knowledge through love, man is re-created into an order that makes a strength of his accepted weakness. After the Fall the highest value is love, by which man fell. The violation of knowledge by love is reconstituted as the ground of possible true knowledge through love. (Though love, through grace and enlarged freedom, transcends obedience, it is not independent of knowledge and the virtues, but is rather the "soul of all the rest" — which would seem to continue the status of soul as agent.)

Love becomes the final symbol of man's limitations and dependence; preliminary symbols were the necessity of Eve and the love that led to the Fall; but now the symbol of man's contingency is *accepted* as his highest value: which leads to the true knowledge of resignation in God's will, to love not of knowledge or of the creature, but through them to love of God. It is a concept of love that comprehends, in a resolution that embraces more of the human and natural, the resolution implied in the paradox of the gnostic *Poemandres*: "and man that hath Mind in him, let him learn to know that he himself is deathless, and that the cause of death is love, though Love is all." [16] Unfallen creatures love God through obeying, the fallen obey through loving. The shift from obedience to love represents the shift from law and knowledge of law to Milton's concept of Christian freedom, which is expressed by the exacting demands of the great injunction: "Thou shalt love the Lord thy God with all thy heart, and with all thy soul, and with all thy mind."

It is a master myth which comprehends future human falls and rebirths, and in the process of working itself out it defines the falseness of anti-myths like Adam's invention to Eve: "if Death / Consort with thee, Death is to mee as Life." Without the drama we might not know the true myth, but the myth finally includes the drama.

ANSWERABLE STYLE

WHEN the Creator viewed the six days' work and saw "all was entirely good," He returned to behold

> how it shew'd
> In prospect from his Throne, how good, how faire,
> Answering his great Idea. (VII, 555ff)

The poet-creator, entirely human in "long choosing, and beginning late," has "this Subject for Heroic Song," and he has "the highth of this great Argument." On a humbler plane he may no doubt have his own "great Idea," to which the whole poem must be answerable. But even the divine Creator will want to view in prospect the answerability of work to Idea; and whether to poet-creator Idea is exactly knowable before being expressed by the work — that is a problem the critic may wisely be busy not to engage. To Milton speculating in prose the poet is a virtuous man and true eloquence, like all noble creation, will return to the pure source which it then will express. One may well think that for a poet with Milton's metaphysical commitments creation would not be conceivable without an Idea, to which the completed poem refers, is potential, and is therefore in some sense subsequent. But having said this, one has not eliminated the fine problems of relationship that remain to trouble metaphysical systems, and for which theology like criticism tends to provide answers from a different order of reasoning. So Milton, in the third chapter of the

Christian Doctrine, says that "prescience can have no influence on the object foreknown, inasmuch as it is only an intransitive action."

My own critical premises make me unwilling to consider seriously Milton's Idea except as it is fully embodied by the completed poem — and then with a consciousness that my consideration is limited and partial. For the poem is itself a created world, an object for contemplation and love, but refusing to yield its final secrets; expressing its great Idea and answerable to reason and love, but supporting the full complexity of creation. The world of the poem requires of the ambitious understanding speculation and recognition of a metaphysical final cause, though that recognition fall short of full understanding of the pure source and its great relationship with every individual but answerable detail. The world of the poem may also be thought of as requiring action of the understanding, in the form of critical statement. I prefer not trying to solve this problem of the creation and the Idea, nor do I wish to insist on my own critical premises any further than may serve to explain my critical deportment.

That Milton himself is aware of the problem is perhaps most evident from his attitude toward the Muse. The poet's Idea can be no pure thought thinking itself; its transcendence expresses itself, according to the truth of its nature, in immanence; as love may be thought to bridge the gap between God and man, the Muse may be thought to bridge the gap between Idea and poet. His Idea must *realize* itself through rising to Subject and Argument, and by the intermediary of Muse. The song is adventurous, what is low in the poet must be raised, what is dark illumined; the verse is easy and unpremeditated, the Muse comes unimplored; but without her aid the poet would be exposed to the harsh influences of time and place. In a practical, "efficient," sense the great Argument is prior to the poet's Idea; though in stricter Platonic terms it is more correct to say that the Idea has prior existence and has been recovered for the individual poet by the Argument.[1] But whatever its exact causal relationship to the Idea, the Argument is also related inextricably to the answerable style:

> If answerable style I can obtaine
> Of my Celestial Patroness.   (IX, 20f)

Milton's style is answerable to the Renaissance concept of epic, which links this poem to classical literature, most particularly perhaps to Virgil. The style must therefore accept the requirements and justify the great privileges of *genus grande*. It must expect to be measured against noble examples, and yet so lofty is the undertaking that any appearance of direct contest will exhibit the personal and flirt with the ridiculous. It must satisfy the expectations of décorum. First of all, an elevation capable of variety must be sustained. In a negative sense this elevation means the purging of the personal, the trivial, the local — yet without exclusion of the natural and simple, or even the purified human voice of the poet himself. In a positive sense this means raising the feelings, mind, and spirit toward a superhuman loftiness beyond any merely immediate and individual passion into a higher unity of experience that can comprehend in its great simplicity of vision, in its terrible yet loving perspective of time and space, all that is various. For variety is also needed; variety of passion, local but not pausing to savor itself; variety of tension, seriousness, even of elevation; variety to make the ultimate unity bearable and true. These requirements, though my exposition may be too personal, were well understood by Milton's contemporaries, and, though there may be differences in emphasis, are, I think, largely accepted by modern scholars. In my approach to Milton's style I shall not try to isolate the Renaissance concept but shall take much of what I have just said for granted.

Milton's style is also answerable to the Renaissance concept of a Christian epic, which links this poem to Scripture, to doctrine, to concepts of biblical style and inspired Christian eloquence held by readers (and nonreaders) of the classics from at least Augustine on. The tradition is a complicated one and I am even less competent to interpret and apply it to Milton than I am the classical concept. So I pass on to my third category, which includes the other two but insists less on competence in advance than on the aspiration to competence. Milton's style is also answerable to the as yet *unattempted*, to the poem this proves to be.

I shall begin with some of the immediate problems that Milton must have had to solve in order to solve his larger problem of building styles into style, variety into unity. It is toward the larger problem that I hope to work.

First there is the question of the dramatic in a poem which presents a large action and many smaller actions, which presents characters in a drama whose scope extends from the domestic to the cosmic. It is plain that the immediate, the local, and the individual cannot be allowed to dominate this epic situation. The stage is too vast — the panorama of hell, heaven, and earth, and their constant relationship. The events are too remote — the climax is on the threshold of time, and only at the end of the poem does the action move in a direct line into our time. (And these considerations must dominate, though there is a vision of history, and there are the frequent intrusive pressures of time, the echoes of the future that reverberate significantly on their source.)

The terms of the drama require that even Satan must realize himself as a public personality; it is not as a person but as a state of mind (however complex and far-reaching in significance) that he must express himself, less in speech than in speeches, and these never delivered without the audible overtones of God's providence. (The diminished Satan of *Paradise Regained* is more nearly individual.) Yet Satan is always interesting as a character; his public personality and his speeches have a liveliness of surface and a richness of depth; he has a history which is always bringing pressure upon the moment, and though the full dramatic illusion would violate the governing principles of this epic, at least there is an immediacy in the *impact* he makes. But if Satan must be presented under these controlling limitations, what of the human pair who are at the center of the drama? Intimations of personality there must be, but shadowed and requiring translation, for only as Adam and Eve approach the Fall can they begin to assume full human personality.

It may seem perverse to apply the term "dramatic" to a situation thus described — especially since visual imagery, colloquial language, and immediacy have usually been regarded by modern critics as indispensable to the "dramatic"; and hostile criticism of Milton has tended to emphasize his lack of these indispensables. Yet Milton plainly conceived of his epic as a great drama; and not merely because he first planned the material as a play; but because as an artist, and indeed as a man, he saw the most significant human experience and human destiny itself as a kind of drama. What the critic must do is obvious — accept Milton's terms and not insist on his own, at least if he wishes to see what Milton has done. And in Milton's kind of dramatic, which would ruin many other fine poems as their kind of dramatic would ruin his, the natural, the familiar, the sharply focused, the completely individual, and all aspects of the immediate must be subordinated to the larger considerations of context, perspective, and to the great order of dynamic interplay which is the total structure.

For instance, in *Paradise Lost* there is a constant and cumulative pressure of local context and its relationship to larger contexts, of local perspective and its relationship to the unfolding perspective which tests, purges, and unites parts into whole. In Milton's art the immediate, however striking it may be, is as likely to contradict as confirm. If it is Satan speaking, for example, there will be the immediate projection of his will, the rhetoric of his present intention; but there will also be a rich interplay of conflicting tensions which connect the most local context (which may be within Satan's own self-contradicting consciousness) with the chain of contexts leading ultimately to God's will. In such an art the elevation of perspective does not inhibit but rather creates variety and interior movement and counter-movement, which in turn test and prove the rightness of the perspective.

Most of these generalizations I have been making are based upon analyses of passages in *Paradise Lost* which I have previously used as arguments for interpretation. I assume that a kind of case for Milton's dramatic style has already been presented; but the issue is important enough to justify some fresh examples directly to the point, in order to illustrate more specifically the way this dramatic style works.

I take Satan's opening speech to Beelzebub, which is introduced by the specific reference to Satan's torment and to the bold words that break the horrid silence — bold in themselves, presumably, and bold because they express a will that can rise above the real terror of the numbing silence. The speech is followed by the choral commentary, "Vaunting aloud, but rackt with deep despare." Introduction and conclusion frame the speech and impose a formal perspective. This may seem to be a blemish and evidence of artistic inadequacy to the critic who regards commentary as the artist's personal intrusion on material that ideally should be able to speak for itself. But such a critical attitude, whatever its merits in other literary situations, can only be misleading here. For one thing, the formal perspective does not force itself upon Satan's speech, does not label and editorialize the impressive willfulness out of existence; but rather sets up a dramatic conflict between the local context of the immediate utterance and the larger context of which the formal perspective is expression. This conflict marks, with a literal accuracy and precision that are dazzling, the tormented relationship between the external boast and the internal despair. (Before he is through with the poem, Milton will have wrung all the rich possibilities for action out of his concept of despair.)

Dramatically, the immediate impact of Satan's great willfulness is more striking than the formal perspective, and this is as it should be; for then if there are small revelations that the external perspective is also expressed *within* the speech, that the despair does betray the boast, we shall have a tension within the speech as well, and the small quiet effects will clash advantageously with the large and loud effects. That is what does happen, and it is no mean dramatic accomplishment. The famous brassy effects come toward the middle of the speech, after Satan has pulled himself together. The opening lines keep trying for Satan's characteristic orchestration and assertiveness of rhythm, but lose their way and falter in a dazed and confused syntax. Mention of the good old cause al-

most regains him his voice, but memory of past and present inter-
feres too violently and shakes loose the stunned surprise that must
have been the shaping force of his first articulation, now finally
stumbling its way into form:

> If thou beest he; But O how fall'n! how chang'd
> From him, who in the happy Realms of Light
> Cloth'd with transcendent brightnes didst outshine
> Myriads though bright: If he whom mutual league,
> United thoughts and counsels, equal hope,
> And hazard in the Glorious Enterprize,
> Joynd with me once, now misery hath joynd
> In equal ruin: into what Pit thou seest
> From what highth fal'n, so much the stronger provd
> He with his Thunder: and till then who knew
> The force of those dire Arms?   (I, 84ff)

In the lines that follow Satan assumes his characteristic style,
which weaves a fine tissue of ironies between Satan's perspective
and God's providence. The boast of "that fixt mind" and "the
unconquerable Will" glitter most and reflect most, but only the
full evolving of the drama under the process of time will reveal
all the particular meanings of the bright refractions. As he concludes his speech, though, the formal perspective which has been
looking over his shoulder, as it were, becomes part of his own
expressed perspective. The movement is subtle, like the skillful
merging of two themes in music; one of them dominating the
other, whether tenderly or gently or patronizingly or harshly, but
with a fine sureness of its own identity. Only here the shaping
skill which is the management of the inner logic of form is not
in Satan's control; he and his consciousness, whatever it may divine of what is happening, act out the drama of the immediate
context without knowing the full relationship of immediate perspective to the whole dramatic plan. Nor do we as readers, but
we see enough to realize that it is drama.

The last two lines of the speech defiantly but ignorantly transfer Satan's own defeated hopes to his description of God, now
triumphantly holding the "Tyranny of Heav'n" alone, and "in
th' excess of joy." The approach to that ending is less defiant, a

somewhat sobered letdown after the earlier largeness of statement. It is presented in the form of causal reasoning, a kind of scrambled syllogism. Since — "by Fate," the metaphysical source which Satan nominates and to which he nominates himself as casual prophet — the "strength" and the "substance" of gods cannot fail; and since, "through experience of this great event," we have lost nothing in arms and have gained in "foresight":

> We may with more successful hope resolve
> To wage by force or guile eternal Warr
> Irreconcileable, to our grand Foe.   (I, 120ff)

It even has a nice internal cross-bolstering: the strength, arms, force lining up to demonstrate the series of unfailing continuance — the argument from soul or will, one might say; and then the more elevated and positive metaphysical argument, presumably from intelligence, the chain of substance, foresight, and guile. This latter series is itself a delicious metaphysical joke, one that comments with independent mischief on the argument, as substance humbly accepts the being of foresight and guile.

There is a rhetorical mischief too, in the disparity between the immediate thundering emphasis of the *eternal* and the *irreconcilable,* and the remarkably shy string of hesitant advances toward the positive committal, which even then still remains governed by the carefully laid down *may*: We may . . . with more . . . successful . . . hope . . . resolve. The formal perspective of despair has permeated the formal logic of the syllogism and acted out the drama of resolved hopelessness founding its hope on the irreconcilable maintenance of that state. The grand defiance of eternal war has quietly excluded the question of possible victory, and Satan has embraced despair as if he were no unwilling victim but an eager lover seeking to prove himself and to learn the nature of the beloved.

This example, though it is especially useful in demonstrating that familiar canons of the dramatic cannot arbitrarily be applied to Milton's style, is by no means unusual. The same basic control of materials, however varied, occurs time and again. Satan, of

course, by nature of his role provides Milton with the best opportunities; the unfallen and still untainted creatures are too nearly
in harmony with the great perspective to admit much conflict.
Adam's first speech (Book IV), for instance, is dignified and
simple, securely removed from the individual and the immediate.
It is pure of internal conflict and yet does not lack external conflict; for it expresses the simplicity of unfallen nature in the great
conflict that is shaping, and it follows immediately after Satan's
fertile demonstration of internal conflict in the "melting" soliloquy that "wonders" at Paradise and man, and dances love and pity
and duty into hatred and self-pity and evasive compulsion.

But Adam's speeches do not remain so simple, nor do Eve's, and
the style — the voice — of each is successfully differentiated from
the other. That is one kind of variety Milton skillfully maintains
within his elevation. The most virtuoso display is, I suppose, that
by the speakers in the Parliament of Hell. There we find stylistic
characterization with broad and heavy strokes — the energetic
stolidity of the die-hard general, the flat language and rhythms of
the business executive. But there are subtly drawn differences too
— as between the rhythms and sensuousness of Satan's first public
speech and those of Belial's oration. Satan puts the pressure of his
personality and feeling and will on every word and rhythm;
Belial starts, at least, by creating the illusion of cool distance, by
the curve of his rhythms, by the graceful syntax of apparently
objective contemplation, though he ends in a sensuousness of attitude and direction that has no object for contemplation but the
deliciousness of self.

God's speeches have hardly aroused critical enthusiasm, though
Milton's skill in providing and adapting biblical phrases has been
admired. Perhaps it is no answer to say that Milton's God is not
presented as a dramatic character. Metaphysically He would seem
to be properly outside the universe of action, though He is also
the biblical God revealing Himself in His chosen terms, however symbolically, to angelic and human understanding. Milton
certainly did not expect his fit audience to read literally, and with
no consciousness of the literary problem of presenting God's

words. (Language and cadence are as unsensuous as if Milton were writing a model for the Royal Society and attempting to speak purely to the understanding.) There at the fountain of light, where there can be no shadow and no reflection, the words themselves can have no overtones or echoes; though after they have been heard and interpreted one may become aware of reflections, less to eye or ear than to understanding, reflections that are the images of the words. The grand style would be presumptuous, and what Milton aims at is a particular kind of bare language that will rise above the familiar associations of such bareness with austerity and harshness. Much, not all, of God's speech is delivered in rhythms that are markedly shorter than usual with Milton, and yet successfully avoid the effects of brokenness or crabbedness. They are no mean achievement of Milton's ear, which has too often received credit for near-perfection at the expense of recognizing the range of its imaginative accomplishments.

Poetry is human and metaphorical, and the Father's speeches are intended to express divine Justice as if directly: to seem without seeming: to create the illusion of no illusion. I pass the problem of trying to judge them — and say only that in Milton's plan it is necessary that God be present and speak; that Justice reveal, however imperfectly in human words, its Idea; which then can be translated perfectly, in the universe where poetry is valid, by the words and actions of God's creatures. The Son is the authorized Word and has the greatest range of speech: He is the Logos creating, the interpreter and declared will of God, He uses "I" gently to Adam and Eve as creator, sternly as judge. He expresses the fullness of divine love, God's "dearest mediation" between eternity and time, immortality and mortality, justice and love.

The scene where He chooses sacrifice in order to fulfill justice is one of Milton's great triumphs of style. Again, all the conflict is external, in what this untroubled simplicity of utterance represents in the whole drama — in the way it will echo when Satan, also "freely," volunteers as individual sacrifice; when Eve chooses the ambitious death of putting off human "to put on Gods" and resolves to share with Adam "all deaths" or "equal Joy, as equal

Love"; when Adam chooses death with Eve, for "Death is to mee as Life"; and when Eve, as the drama moves into the myth of redemption, prays that all the *sentence* fall on her; and Adam, in the forgiveness of renewed love and the acceptance of justice, gently says that if prayers could alter high decrees he would, first and more loudly, pray "That on my head all might be visited." The Son's speech has no internal conflict, for it is above human drama. But it expresses the divine order against which conflict is free to try itself — the expression of justice in terms of the immortal love for the mortal. It speaks with grace and beauty and purity to human senses, as the sanctioned mediation between the human metaphor of poetry and reality:

> Father, thy word is past, man shall find grace;
> And shall grace not find means, that finds her way,
> The speediest of thy winged messengers,
> To visit all thy creatures, and to all
> Comes unprevented, unimplor'd, unsought,
> Happie for man, so coming; he her aide
> Can never seek, once dead in sins and lost;
> Attonement for himself or offering meet,
> Indebted and undon, hath none to bring:
> Behold mee then, mee for him, life for life
> I offer, on mee let thine anger fall;
> Account mee man; I for his sake will leave
> Thy bosom, and this glorie next to thee
> Freely put off, and for him lastly die
> Well pleas'd, on me let Death wreck all his rage . . .
>
> (III, 227ff)

The narrative and descriptive, which must bulk large in an epic, are also capable of conveying patterns of movement and conflict, so we must consider some properties of style that exist independent of direct speech. Milton's diction, his imagery, and his management of structures of sound all present separate problems in the larger problem of describing his style. The separate problems are not confined to the single problem of the dramatic, though it is convenient to study them in this connection.

Milton's diction is both carefully elevated and sensitively graduated. Without the elevation — the abstract level which must be created by the poet, built up and concretely maintained — his range would be far smaller, and he would not be able to use the reader's expectation as a constant by which to secure some very precise effects. This management of the levels of diction is a great technical accomplishment that deserves more extensive study than the present approach permits; but like all details of Milton's technique the final justification, whatever the rich immediate rewards, lies in the answerability of the style. (If the rewards are rich they are also necessary — in accordance with the tangible terms of Milton's concept of the human drama: which concept accords well with the relationship between freedom and necessity within the world which any great work of art creates. This is at the moment perhaps too serious a point to make, but it is a reminder that our chief subject is the unity of Milton's style.) The management of the diction is in effect much like the management of perspective in speeches or in narrative and descriptive passages. As we have already noted, when Satan resolves *eternal* and *irreconcilable* war he has significantly shifted his diction from the less positive level of "We may with more successful hope."

Even the generalized and the remote, twentieth-century readers apparently need reminding, may be more than an empty ceremony of elevation. When Eve, on the fateful morning, drops her formal address and calls Adam by his plain name, she presages her shocking change in style and status — to the completely individualized diction, accents, and rhythm of the naturally human; one might say, of the merely human as recorded in scenes of stage comedy. After the reconciliation, but most signally in the very last lines of the poem, the diction (though not that alone of course) restores them to a human dignity that accepts (and is expressed in the verse) both what was *individual* in their error and *universal* in its consequences. They are naturally human but not merely so, for they are both fallen and raised; if they let drop some "natural tears," it is not for long, since the whole world — remote, grand, terrible, exciting — lies before them; and their great new adventure, anticipated in vision but still to be experi-

enced, is at once the loss of their old freedom and the gain of
their new freedom, with Providence their guide and the harsh
immediacies of time mitigated by the known promise of eternity.

We remember our first view:

> So passd they naked on, nor shund the sight
> Of God or Angel, for they thought no ill:
> So hand in hand they passd.   (IV, 319ff)

That is the simple grandeur of unfallen dignity seen as a whole,
without individualizing physical detail; as from an indeterminate
distance in which they move with an absolute evenness of pro-
gression that forces us to see only their wholeness, and nothing
more individual than the added "hand in hand" as our mind returns, from having contemplated the intellectual-spiritual source
of their physical dignity, to the view of the sustained progress
our eyes have never left.

And our last view:

> They hand in hand with wandring steps and slow,
> Through *Eden* took thir solitarie way.   (XII, 648f)

This view is also one of wholeness, of two figures viewed as one
in the distance; now no longer indeterminate but located in the
dimension of time between a past already realized and a future
promised in vision; and located between the tragic drama of
human experience already realized yet still to be realized again
and again; and between part of the myth of God's providential
order already realized by them in their redemption, but still to
be finally realized beyond the invisibly lighted horizon toward
which they move, as the eastern gate of Paradise becomes their
west, now dreadfully illuminated in the sunset-dawn of human
time. But to say that our final view is located is not to say that it
is concretely immediate, or to say that the diction is not generalized and remote, not kept pure of active metaphor and specific
association: all of which sounds like a twentieth-century recipe
for bad poetry.

More of that in a moment and a little longer on these lines —
since I am letting this example stand for a quality that is pure in

very many of Milton's lines and a significant part of his whole style. The language is familiar and simple but not *natural*, though the action deliberately presented is breath-taking in its naturalness *and* in its deliberate presentation — *and* in the relationship established between the two. Neither language nor rhythm is based on the colloquial; the words are carefully chosen to avoid *freshness*; they are literary, made familiar by Milton's poem and now elevated by rhythm and context and by the accumulating weight of the experience behind them. Words and rhythms echo and recapitulate but stiffen and turn straight out with the "took" that announces the new life of choosing; at "solitary" the echoes reverberate for a moment until the firm line of the rhythm and the more recent memories assert themselves and make the pathos bearable, together and under hope; while the surroundings drop undistinguishably back from them.

Mr. Eliot in his 1947 lecture on Milton speaks of the negative rules that can be learned from some great poets: "They teach us what to avoid, by showing us what great poetry can do without — how *bare* it can be." [2] This seems to refer to a long-standing ideal of the critic and the poet; witness Matthiessen's quotation from an unpublished lecture of 1933:

This speaks to me of that at which I have long aimed, in writing poetry; to write poetry which should be essentially poetry, with nothing poetic about it, poetry standing naked in its bare bones, or poetry so transparent that we should not see the poetry, but that which we are meant to see through the poetry, poetry so transparent that in reading it we are intent on what the poem *points at*, and not on the poetry, this seems to me the thing to try for. To get beyond poetry, as Beethoven, in his later works, strove to get *beyond music*. [3]

That aim, and some of the phrases, will be familiar to readers of his *Quartets*, who will recognize that more is meant, or intended, than the good old-fashioned aim of art to conceal art.

Apparently there is bareness and bareness, for Milton *is* different, as admirers of Dante seem to agree. Perhaps his difference lies in his major commitment to, his full acceptance of, this world, his refusal to strip down for, to point his poem toward another world: call it sensuous, or baroque, or the results of a different theology, the other side of his mortalism; or perhaps his mortalism is the necessary other side of this. But there is a poetic difference too. As Allen Tate has said in a pertinent side comment,[4] the great masters of a period style (as Johnson, or Eliot and Pound) have created their own worthy obstacles between them and another period style. Mr. Eliot regards Milton the poet as "probably the greatest of all eccentrics" — and the "peculiar greatness" is located in the "violence" Milton does to language by writing "poetry at the farthest possible remove from prose."[5] This would seem to me most nearly relevant to Milton's deliberately ornate verse, to the rich exploitations of language that are perhaps most frequent in hell or where extreme virtuosity is required by the argument, sometimes as a case for simplicity. It would be quite irrelevant to some of the passages, admittedly rare, in which we hear poetry pitched close to prose in the manner now familiar to us through Donne and much recent poetry:

> Let us not then pursue
> By force impossible, by leave obtain'd
> Unacceptable, though in Heav'n, our state
> Of splendid vassalage, but rather seek
> Our own good from our selves, and from our own
> Live to our selves, though in this vast recess,
> Free, and to none accountable. (II, 249ff)

Here Mammon gives us, with the possible exception of two ringing phrases, the broken argumentative rhythms of Donne or Greville; as Satan does in part of his speech to Eve:

> I question it, for this fair Earth I see,
> Warm'd by the Sun, producing every kind,
> Them nothing: If they all things, who enclos'd
> Knowledge of Good and Evil in this Tree . . . (IX, 720ff)

But these passages do not *represent* Milton and they are peripheral to his answerable style because he needed a style he could easily *descend* from, not *rise* from. The difference between Milton, even when he is most simple in his language, and what I assume

Mr. Eliot to have in mind is that Milton apparently does not try to get beyond poetry. Milton has a Muse, and it would perhaps not do for him to pretend otherwise. But the difference is not in the fact of ritual, it is in the kind, for Mr. Eliot has his own highly developed rituals — the results of which I am not backward in admiring.

Even the "bareness" of Milton's great hymn to light is that of the poet singing — under the auspices of Muse and theme. It is not less impersonal because the poet is there, performing the office of his mystery and being absorbed into it as part of it; but that is his role and not the illusion of not being there at all.

> Thus with the Year
> Seasons return, but not to me returns
> Day, or the sweet approach of Ev'n or Morn,
> Or sight of vernal bloom, or Summers Rose,
> Or flocks, or herds, or human face divine;
> But cloud in stead, and ever-during dark
> Surrounds me, from the chearful waies of men
> Cut off . . .   (III, 40ff)

One sees interesting differences if one puts beside these lines the beautiful lyric from the sixth section of "Ash Wednesday":

> And the lost heart stiffens and rejoices
> In the lost lilac and the lost sea voices
> And the weak spirit quickens to rebel
> For the bent golden-rod and the lost sea smell
> Quickens to recover
> The cry of quail and the whirling plover . . .

In both passages the words and what they represent are refined to an essential simplicity. But one must distinguish by adding that Mr. Eliot's objects are deliberately more individual (no doubt more personal) and intended to invoke the universal partly through the acuteness and force with which the particulars are presented; so that once they are presented the immediacy of the particulars disappears in the timelessness of the experience, and perhaps one may then say that the poetry itself becomes the state it creates and so we get beyond the poetry. To that end Mr.

Eliot's individual details contribute, because they are not every man's but are capable of becoming every man's during the moment of transformation, after which they will better disappear because they *are* individual and produced by no inevitable human pattern. (If I were discussing the lines that immediately follow, I should have to qualify this further.) To that end the rhythm contributes, beautifully formed as it is upon a model of colloquial speech; and the order and syntax unroll like simple modest prose offering what it says as if without itself.

And Milton's lines? They are *sung*, in the measured liberty of the iamb, which has its affinity to speech rhythm, but here formally forces speech to sing and refuses to permit simple words and phrases, so natural to prose, to become prose. The "gentle" violence of the meter is added to by the syntax, which is poetic; it may be Coleridge's "logic of passion or universal logic" but certainly it is not prose syntax. One could read Mr. Eliot's lines as prose, flattening out the music and slurring the tempo, but keeping the accents pretty intact; and something decent would be left. Milton's lines would be impossible as prose, intolerable in syntax and order and rhythm. Milton's particulars seem hardly more individual than the summer's rose, which in this context is almost bold. They are not there to disappear, any more than meter or syntax; they *are* every man's particulars and celebrate the basic joys of sight in the prospect of loss.

The normal, everyday, natural experience of man, which can be wonderfully taken for granted — that is now celebrated as wonderful fact by the bare inventory, but the heightened voice, as each item is rediscovered in the loving definition of loss. The miraculous items of the normal are rediscovered and defined almost as essences. Since the experience begins by being timeless, and the items fulfill an inevitable pattern of human expectation, no considerable transformation of individual details is needed. Or one might say that in this art, which can depend on art and on certain undamaged human potentialities, there is no need for the poetry to create from start to finish almost the whole cycle of creating the state and then becoming it. This is not to say that one poet creates his state and the other invokes his, ready-made as it were; the truth lies somewhere between, and the distinction perhaps cannot be made at all without exaggeration.

From Milton's perspective of loss we are in a world surrounded and cut off from the natural world of cycle and change, of return and approach. Qualifying epithets, though no more finely discriminated than to designate seasons, carry unusual weight, and so does the mere naming of evening and morning, those luxurious refinements of the miracle of day. The rose almost violates the experience – by carrying the broad gradations of variety to an almost unbearable extreme of the specific. And *sweet*, that adjective as common as day, is more startling than the rose and moves further in the same direction. There at the *approach* to the border of change, when all the senses are especially eager to do what they are supposed to do, the failure of the returned approach is particularly associated with sweetness. But morning and evening can be smelled and heard and tasted, even felt, as all the senses combine to *feel about* the time, to experience, and to draw together all the apprehended qualities – and that whole composite feeling, experience and literature prove, may be associated with sweetness. (We may remember the sweetness of times, particularly mornings, in Paradise.) But the general quality of sweetness, often so comprehensive as to deny discrimination, is here limited to the one specific faculty of sight. By contrast, this unexpected particularization of a general term in a context remarkable for its pattern of inevitability, introduces an intensity of the individual that counterpoints, to say the least, every man's re-experiencing of the basic joys of sight in the prospect of loss. For a moment the loss *almost* becomes immediate and personal, the poet speaking as John Milton the man.

Perhaps I have labored the point and can say it more simply. Where we should expect a general term without reverberation or surprise we get what is really a specific term, and that clashes momentarily against the larger pattern of the experience. For what it is worth, this discrimination seems possible: in Milton's lines the impersonal and universal strain toward the individual and personal, but within the freedom of discipline and measure, which assert the universal; in Eliot's lines the personal and individual move under their own discipline toward the impersonal and universal. Milton, at least, neither tries to nor gets beyond poetry.

Though basic problems of art have not changed since Milton's time, some differences must be noted. The modern poet has felt more necessity to create everything in motion, ideas, doctrine, style — to win his vision, if he does, out of daylight materials before the very eyes of spectator and performer. This has meant, in Mr. Eliot's words, "that verse should have the virtues of prose, that diction should become assimilated to cultivated contemporary speech, before aspiring to the elevation of poetry." [6] Neither this statement nor the best practice subscribes very seriously to any doctrine of naturalism, but rather to purgation and a new start under new standards to be discovered by ear and by eye. The standard of contemporary speech is not to be minimized, but neither is it a complete standard nor is it arrived at only through itself. "Cultivated" implies history. Poets have sharpened their ears for contemporary speech by sharpening their ears for some of the older poetry. Nor is the result without some local, some period phenomena. Coleridge and Wordsworth, faced with the same problem and admiring the language of some of the same poets, did not find that language available to them as poets.

Milton does not have to begin from scratch, or think he ought to, or conceal his presence or his premises. He has a complete mastery of the known devices of rhetoric and an enormous capacity for inventing his own — nor is this an art to disguise with shame, if the mastery can be presumed to take care of itself, with the false and rotten nicely revealed (in delight) and the noble not requiring apology, or the recommendation of the natural, or the illusion of having just been created. He could have subscribed wholeheartedly to Ben Jonson's dictum:

As it is a great point of art, when our matter requires it, to enlarge and veer out all sail, so to take it in and contract it is of no less praise, when the argument doth ask it. [7]

And he would have seen the partial relevance between human art and Sir Thomas Browne's remark about divine art:

For God is like a skilful geometrician, who, when more easily and with one stroke of his compass he might describe or divide a right line, had yet rather do this in a circle or longer way, according to the constituted and fore-laid principles of his art.[8]

Language, to a Milton nurtured in the Renaissance, is God-given, and still capable of revealing authentic relationship with its origin; capable of corruption, of charming for better or worse both sense and soul; but also capable of being correlative to the true thought in the mind. As Satan bears unwilling witness in *Paradise Regained:*

> Thy actions to thy words accord, thy words
> To thy large heart give utterance due, thy heart
> Conteins of good, wise, just, the perfect shape.   (III, 9ff)

"Custom is the most certain mistress of language": here again Ben Jonson sums up opinion. But custom, general opinion back of Jonson would suggest, is most nearly absolute ruler only in determining such minor matters as accent; in all the finer determinations of meaning and usage, in the creation of new words and revival of old, in the recovery of latent meanings, in the management of words — custom is what the best judges approve, "the consent of the learned; as custom of life, which is the consent of the good."[9]

For Milton the sources of the eloquent and the good are in a return to nature, but unfallen nature. For Milton the grand masterpiece of decorum is easily available and workable, and so are a tradition of valid concepts and a tradition of dramatic and mythic thought and expression. And he has available a literary language of unparalleled richness, with a tradition of flexibility and fertility, still capable of delighting both in the unexhausted metaphorical resources of old words and in the taste of new words. He profits perhaps from the severe linguistic criteria of the new science, but in the interest of deliberate precision, without surrendering faith in metaphor, in the larger miracles to which the little miracles of words are still an authentic vehicle. Language is to be watched and tested and disciplined, as all man's gifts, but to be trusted too. Though Milton's language is consciously literary and far removed from everyday prose, it is nevertheless not cut off from what Yeats calls "that spoken word which knits us to normal man . . . our delight in the whole man." Milton does not have to worry about the peculiar problems of language corrupted by mass communication, or debunked by scientific and philosophic analysis, or elevated by primitivizers of various casts, naturalistic and symbolic, opposing the pure liberating experience and wisdom of word-thing to the tyranny of ideas.

If Milton seems such an "eccentric" with words it is partly because he doesn't have to think *about* his language. For all his consciousness as an artist Milton must have been pretty well able to let his art take care of itself while he listened to the easy dictation of his Muse. The great freedom he enjoys is the perquisite of the discipline he has mastered, the responsibility he has accepted. He can think *through* his language, and achieve his own transparency, which is the perfection of decorum, the great weight of tradition drawn into the uniqueness of immediate and total answerability — and he can do this because he has brought his language thoroughly to the service of his whole consciousness. He is under no more compulsion to try to get beyond poetry than Bach to get beyond music.

I now turn to some problems in Milton's management of structures of sound, and by this phrase, instead of some version of the more familiar "Miltonic music," I intend to indicate my attitude. To the student of contemporary criticism the most unexpected, and even radical, remark in Mr. Eliot's later essay on Milton ought to be the last phrase of the following: "The emphasis is on the sound, not the vision, upon the word, not the idea; and in the end it is the unique versification that is the most certain sign of Milton's intellectual mastership." [10]

F. R. Leavis is left quite bewildered, and small wonder; for to him response to the Miltonic music "is a relaxation of attentiveness to sense." [11] And indeed the whole practice of most of the best of modern criticism, under the joint influence of T. S. Eliot and I. A. Richards, has been solidly on the side of sense in poetry. Versification has been largely taken for granted by critics, with the notable exceptions of Yvor Winters and John Crowe Ransom. It has been common agreement of course that style should not be separated from content, and that has no doubt led to our improved understanding of the sense of the content and the sense of the style.

But there have been disadvantages too, in our not having persistently enough studied elements of style that do not readily come under a category of sense. And the result has been some tendency to make style a function of content, even while assuming that a "functional" theory of art protects the critic from the familiar dilemmas of an esthetic dualism. At the worst, one may have a merely functional concept limiting art to the service of the practical: which I take to be the extreme opposite of the metaphysical concept implied in Sir Thomas Browne's remark, quoted above, on the art of God. But even when that extreme is not intended, one may see what has been widely demonstrated: that in warmly pursuing the trail of a structure of meaning one may nod politely to the rich circumstances of texture but recognize only what is to the purposes of structure. And this leads some critics to make rather flimsy remarks about alliterative and rhythmic effects — not at all on a level with the perceptions they win from their more strenuous disciplines of analysis: for these disciplines are methods to a goal in which they believe, while the flimsy remarks are incidental by-products and to be kept only when useful to the main purpose. I think this objection applies also to the study of imagery (without denying Aristotle on metaphor, or challenging the main claims of modern extensions) — when the study of imagery is offered as if it satisfied all the claims of style.

The danger is that the style described exclusively in terms of the same categories of sense that apply to content (structure) is a style that has by critical practice been reduced conceptually to a dependent role of illustration, that *imitates* the structure. And this would lead the critic, by an unanticipated direction, into the heresy he is committed to abhor, that of separating thought from expression. I am not entirely convinced that the heresy has not been somewhat superficially considered, and used as an argument more beholden to the times than to truth. But I pass that point. Nor do I propose a solution, or even an alternative more radical than increased critical consciousness. The problem is complex and my aim is not theoretical.

The causes of this attitude and emphasis are in part, it seems clear, involved in twentieth-century reactions against the poetry and criticism of the preceding era. The issues, though new in their formulation, have a long history. Of most relevance to our present concern is the late sixteenth-century distinction between sound and sense in language, a distinction that likewise reacts against one poetry and prose and serves as program for another. The revolution in style begun there soon calls for the common language of artisans in preference to the language of scholars; and identifies the sense of words with the soul, sometimes in order to scorn as body (in a paradoxical Platonizing of science) whatever does not conform with a fixed idea of sense. (Milton, one should not be surprised to note, is hardly to be tempted into accepting such a division between verbal soul and matter; he has already worked out this problem to his satisfaction, and on a more ambitious plane of thought.)

The modern emphasis on the colloquial and on sense is disposed to maintain a suspicious guard against fine sounds, in spite of some notable modern and Renaissance examples of irresistible magniloquence. The critic will seem least uneasy when he can reduce an effect of sound to an already recognized effect of sense. Perhaps that is why the passages from Milton that F. R. Leavis quotes with approval are likely to be examples of a kind of literary program music, where the sound echoes the sense by imitating it. For instance, the early lines mentioning the ejection of Satan from heaven, the brilliant episode of the "Hurld headlong flaming." Or the lively and "Elizabethan" speech by Comus tempting the Lady, at its very best in the wonderful line about the silkworms, "That in their green shops weave the smooth-hair'd silk."

Mr. Leavis, however, pursues the sense of poetry more strenuously than Donald R. Roberts, whose study of Milton's music is founded on Pope's shallow formula of the sound as echo of the sense. Thus conceived, it is a limited sense which can be imitated or suggested by the sound — for the most part rather general physical states or actions. According to Mr. Roberts something more than the example of poetry is needed to explain Milton's great mastery of the imitative effects which are "a vital and essential part of Milton's poetic technique . . . an integral element of his art." He finds a source in Renaissance music, in the drawn-out and varied effects of madrigal and motet, but particularly in the naturalistic imitations of Monteverdi: "The poet seeks to fit the melody, as well as the rhythm, of his words to the immediate sensuous impression or association that is to be conveyed, sometimes with some concomitant sacrifice of the intellectual element." [12] Mr. Roberts, I think, is far more preoccupied with the immediate and "musical" impression than the poet is, and he misconstrues many passages because he does not consider the whole situation which governs the role of the immediate impression. Any concept of the "intellectual element" which does not take account of Milton's management of perspective is, as I trust we have already seen, inadequate and so distorting.

The problem, to face it directly and present my own demonstration, is a difficult one. It deserves ambitious treatment as an aspect of *harmony*, and Milton's larger esthetic achievement. But what I intend now is a more modest attempt to examine some of the relationship between Milton's sound and sense. I begin by saying, since I have recently published a similar study of Donne, that Milton's patterns of sound are more difficult to analyze than Donne's. Milton's basic rhythm is more horizontal; the emphasis corresponds less obviously to a rhetoric of sharply defined metrical stresses; there is a far greater sensuousness, for *copia*, for the flow and sweep of heightened bigness; and patterns of sound are used with great confidence to shape and modulate metaphorical meaning. As I have already suggested, the cause is no doubt to be traced to Milton's poetic metaphysics, to his refusal to make a ruinous division between verbal soul and matter. But this is the kind of problem better treated, though inadequately, by modest example than by ambitious statement.

There *is* some naturalistic imitation in *Paradise Lost*, more than Mr. Leavis and less than Mr. Roberts thinks. It may convey, though perhaps by a use of language that Mr. Eliot could not countenance, an immediacy of physical action. For instance, the crowd of angels who rush into completed Pandemonium and are discriminated only by whether they praise the work or the architect: "The hasty multitude / Admiring enter'd." Their jostling mass and their articulating blur of enthusiasm seem to precede their actual entrance, which is an illusion true to the nature of such a crowd. The trick is also deliberate illusion — the transfers of epithet and syntax, the extravagant mouthing necessary to read the words — and meant to be comic. I think it has not been noted how often Milton's naturalistic imitations deliberately transfer their excess to the immediate situation, as a kind of dramatic device by which an action or a situation is given a characterizing voice. It is a particularly useful device for giving the qualities of a spoken part to description; and since it almost always seems a little extravagant, it is best suited for humor, and is capable of rather subtle gradations. After Satan has been subjected to his first extended view of the beauties of Paradise and the human inhabitants, the narrative voice returns to him. The first line describes him as still fixed, which reminds one of the internal conflict that has apparently been continuing between the preceding soliloquy and the one about to begin. The line itself is not particularly emphatic in its expression of fixedness; but the rather mechanical sequence of stresses perhaps suggests a kind of numbness, and does underline the extraordinary near-collapse of rhythm as the second line mischievously imitates the shocked physical and psychological condition of Satan:

When *Satan* still in gaze, as first he stood,
Scarce thus at length faild speech recoverd sad.   (IV, 356f)

The effect is most likely to be comic when the imitation attempts to be quite complete, and for the most part when Milton is using the device seriously he follows the sound rhetorical principle that the good metaphor comes limping. (In his prose, for satiric purposes, he sometimes deliberately pushes a metaphorical correspondence to ludicrous extremes — as unsuccessful metaphysical poets sometimes do unwittingly.) For instance, the following serious example, the echoed line which closes Book X: "in sign / Of sorrow unfeign'd, and humiliation meek." Neither action nor psychological state is exactly imitated. But the two parts of the line are sharply contrasted, in sound as well as meaning. The first part is more emphatic, physically open and demonstrative in effect. The climax is loudly upon "unfeigned," which rings out its vowels unhindered by the consonants but rather assisted; while the consonants of "sorrow" are quite unemphatic, leaving the first syllable open and not sharply formed and allowing the second syllable to elide into the next word. The second part of the line is sharply defined in its consonants and kept at a low, level, and unemphatic movement in its rhythm. This pattern of sound does not correspond with the action or psychological state, but with a moral concept of behavior that lies behind the immediate texture of the line. For the sorrow of repentance must be unfeigned and expressive to be genuine and single, to thrust beyond the inner complexities of the personal, and to purge in an initial and general way. But the humiliation must be restrained and unexpressive, meek and externally undistinguished. To test negatively one may see what happens by making the sorrow meek and the humiliation unfeigned.

This kind of example seems to me far more important for understanding Milton's metrical style than the more brilliant virtuosity that opens gates jarringly or melodiously, and the like. The basic point to make, in any case, is that the pattern of sound does not reinforce an already established meaning so much as it helps shape and modulate that meaning. The point is worth emphasizing because of the great fuss that has been made about the beautiful *vagueness* of Milton's sounds. Mr. Roberts, for instance, quotes from Adam's account of his creation, "And liquid Lapse of murmuring Streams." To see this only as an imitation of liquidity is not to see much. The liquid and the murmuring are the ready coin of poesy; the *lapse* bears Milton's authentic stamp. Whatever it suggests by way of sound (including the pun), one ought not miss the fact that Adam is *seeing* the water and that the sound of the water owes something to the very exact meaning of lapse — the falling, running downward movement, discontinuous within the continuous, that causes the liquid murmuring.

Or consider this purple passage that announces the decision of the great debate in Pandemonium:

> With Trumpets regal sound the great result:
> Toward the four winds four speedy Cherubim
> Put to thir mouths the sounding Alchymie
> By Haralds voice explain'd: the hollow Abyss
> Heard farr and wide, and all the host of Hell
> With deafning shout, return'd them loud acclaim.
>
> (II, 515ff)

The first line convincingly imitates the abrupt punctuation and the carrying blare of the trumpets — by rhythmic emphasis, by the vowel tones, and the consonantal clusters (tr–t, r–g, gr–t, r–t; and also the necessary spit of the *s*, the brassy gurgle of the *l*, and the tongued stop of the *the*). This brilliant display of sound effects marks with flourishes the disparity between the substance and the announcement of the result, and mocks the gaudy pomp with which hell imitates the *state* of heaven. The "alchemy," which Raleigh strangely thought an epic circumlocution to avoid with a pretty word and sound the vulgar naming of an instrument, is both the actual metal made by alchemists for trumpets and the familiar fraud of the alchemists' unachieved result. The "explained," as rhythm and sound, is propelled outward with great energy and then sustained in a widening sound one seems to hear carrying on during the interval, which seems relatively long, before one can rhythmically resume the line; and what follows ("the hollow Abyss") is lower in pitch and rhythmic intensity: which allows the preceding climax to be heard yet, or at least felt as an unsilenced force, *over* the lower pitch and intensity. (The effect is more common in music, where it may also be a created illusion, but can as well be an actual effect of orchestration.)

With the next line we have resumed the sustained and widening sound. The impulse of sound we heard carrying outward is now heard, with a similar intensity of rhythm and high pitch, on the far extremities. First we seem to be at the source hearing it, and then as the sound moves into the distance we follow, overtake, and anticipate, without having quite lost it from our ears during the transition. Then we hear, from the far distance, the sound come and spread and return to the angels standing in the middle distance, as it were. They, like the hollow abyss, collect the sound during an interval of lowered pitch and rhythmic intensity ("and all the host of Hell"), and return it to the source. It is not quite the same sound, one should note; for the distance is much less and the mass of the volume greater, so that one hears the final sound only as a totally enveloping choral chord, with no sense of linear dimension. One should also note that the final vowel of "acclaim" repeats that of "explained" — and this vowel sound has been carefully omitted in all the circular development that carries through the low pitch of "The hollow Abyss," the high pitch, but altered, of "Heard farr and wide," the low pitch of "and all the host of Hell," and the mounting tones of the last line. The fact of the initial and final *l*'s, the final *m*'s, and the connecting *h*'s I note but pass by.

Unless I have erred badly, the pattern of sound just described is no music of beautiful vagueness and does not, of its own nature, encourage a relaxed "attentiveness to sense." Nor does it convey only an "immediate sensuous impression." The sounds do not reinforce rhetorically an established image, nor do they merely make alive and persuasive an image that is in any satisfactory sense prior and defined. The pattern of sounds is largely responsible for the dramatic immediacy which is created; but to stop with that conclusion is to see the pattern again as a kind of rhetorical device used for a calculated aim. If one insists on seeing the full role of the sounds in the image, one must recognize that the sounds shape the image creatively. In this sense, the sounds may with no more accuracy be called naturalistic imitation than the image itself. For one thing, the familiar precedents of naturalistic imitation are all far simpler in effect — usually limited to the kind of state, or action, or aspect of an action that the sensuous can successfully imitate or caricaturize. Here the physical action is complex and involves psychological action as well. Part of the complexity and the precision of the image is dependent on details that are nonnaturalistic. Most obvious is the elaborate "musical" structure from "explained" to "acclaim."

But take the word "explained." The customary meaning would neither contradict nor justify, but could accommodate, the description of its effect as sound. What Milton has done here is release the original metaphor, with its physical and psychological action, upon which the derived meaning is based. Compared with the more primitive meaning, the derived meaning tends to be abstract, the accepted equivalent of the familiar result or even process of an action, but with no physical or imaginative sense of the very happening of that process. The sound of the word, as Milton uses it here, justifies and is thoroughly involved in the etymologically older meaning of flatten out and so make *plain*. But whatever naturalistic origin may be furnished for this word or other words, the poet returning to an older meaning, even when he re-creates that meaning sensuously in the context, still owes something to what has become an unnatural usage, though sanctioned by art and history. The poet who exploits the imitative potentialities of such a word can do so, whatever he owes to the relationship between the primitive and the poetic, only as a scholar of words writing to scholars of words. Perhaps this is where one should stop, or start, by recognizing the full involvement of sound and meaning. My speculation on this word leads me back to my starting point: the best way to understand the pattern of sound here is as a shaping and integral part of the created image.

But I must look back a moment longer. For all its intensive and extensive particularity of detail, the pattern of sound just examined has more in common with that of the line, "Of sorrow unfeign'd, and humiliation meek," than with the patterns in lines that intend to be more completely imitative — say, for example, the virtuoso effects that introduce the comic reduction in size, in the hall of Pandemonium, of the minor angels: "Brusht with the hiss of russling wings." Though the physical process of the "explained" is conjured up with a loving accuracy of sensuousness, that accuracy does not exist entirely for its own sake, but it focuses the process and it limits — toward a structure of meaning that is embodied in the immediate texture but extends beyond. (Similarly, the less complex pattern of sound in "Of sorrow unfeign'd, and humiliation meek" corresponds to an underlying concept of behavior.) And part of the effect of the limiting is to prevent any merely sensuous response by a reader relaxing to the soft focus of large swirls of undiscriminated feeling. The sensuous precision is here as considerable as the intellectual precision; and both demand a wide-awake apprehension of the context, the sounding alchemy and the great result, and of the whole process as a magnificent illusion — with the echo amplified by the physical and the psychological-political surfaces, returning in greater volume than the initial sound. It is an illusion that the fallen angels participate in, while we both participate and observe. So the structure of sound here corresponds both to an immediate structure of meaning and to a larger structure of meaning. It shapes the image, but it shapes it intellectually, just as the intellectually perceivable meaning of "explained" shapes the structure of sound.

Let us now consider some examples that will demonstrate less but are somewhat easier to deal with. First, this description of Adam:

> and Hyacinthin Locks
> Round from his parted forelock manly hung
> Clustring, but not beneath his shoulders broad.
>
> (IV, 301 ff)

The pattern of sounds here sets up the limits and direction of the image — Adam's manly beauty, which must be seen as neither too "manly" nor too "beautiful." See what happens by substituting "clustered" for "clustering." An already strong and hard rhythm that helps keep the beauty masculine would lose a small but necessary grace, and by that little difference the masculinity would tend too much to harshness and austerity. Or rearrange the line thus: Hung manly from his parted forelock round. That would be to turn the hardness into softness, very dangerously, in spite of what the words say.

Consider the following examples, where the pattern of sounds performs a similar limiting office but shapes both a direction and a counterdirection. First, the departure of Sin and Death through chaos:

> Then Both from out Hell Gates into the *w*aste
> *W*ide Anarchie of Chaos *d*amp and *d*ark
> Fle*w d*ivers.   (X, 282ff)

The rhythmic impulse of the *w*–*w* is upward and outward, of the *d*–*d* downward. The final *w*–*d*, if it represents anything, is certainly different; the *w* is less upward and the *d* less downward; if they have not reversed their directions they have at least compromised them, perhaps under the influence of chaos. Another example is the brief picture of Sin that introduces her motion to come between Satan and Death:

> the Snakie Sorceress that sat
> Fast by Hell Gate.   (II, 724f)

Here the writhing motion of the foreground against the immobile mass of the background owes a good deal to the relationship of *s* and *t*. One more example, somewhat more involved, is the account of the birth of Sin:

> All on a sudden miserable pain
> Surpris'd thee, dim thine eyes, and dizzie swumm
> In darkness, while thy head flames thick and fast
> Threw forth.   (II, 752ff)

The movement is both strongly forward and strongly circular, and corresponds in a remarkable way to both the physical act of the birth and the symbolic act of the birth of sin. Satan's state is

involuntary, "surprised" (in the double sense of being taken unexpectedly and taken completely, *astonished*), in a kind of physical
and spiritual vertigo that turns him, involuted, about himself. At
the same time a countermotion is violently eruptive; that too is
involuntary, now, but it is like the Aristotelian ethical distinction,
the involuntary but necessary result of what once was a voluntary choice. The rhythm, mounting emphatically on the *d*'s rises
forward to the climax, but is suspended by the syntax. The final
f's and *th*'s interweave, like the darkness and flame, and the birth
is expelled out of the flames enveloping the head, as the final
propulsive thrust of the "threw forth" bursts out of the suspended
involution.

These demonstrations seem to me to speak for themselves, even
after the errors and personal distortions of the analysis have been
discounted. (I am under no illusion that I have been entirely
accurate or complete, though I hope I have been clear and definite.) On the basis of what these examples show I am going to
pass up any direct consideration of Milton's visual imagery. For,
to speak practically, I am not attempting a full description of
Milton's style, and certainly no catalogue. But perhaps one convenient example may serve to illustrate some of the relationship
between Milton's imagery and the kind of hard-focused imagery
now usually called "visual." It is the passage describing the creation of fish:

> Forthwith the Sounds and Seas, each Creek & Bay
> With Frie innumerable swarme, and Shoales
> Of Fish that with thir Finns & shining Scales
> Glide under the green Wave, in Sculles that oft
> Bank the mid Sea: part single or with mate
> Graze the Sea weed thir pasture, & through Groves
> Of Coral stray, or sporting with quick glance
> Show to the Sun thir wav'd coats dropt with Gold,
> Or in thir Pearlie shells at ease, attend
> Moist nutriment.   (VII, 399ff)

It is all vague and under water. Only when the fish break the
surface do we have for a moment a defined picture — "thir wav'd

coats dropt with Gold." But one visualizes — that is, imagines — the fish, and the vagueness helps, especially the combination of vagueness and the sudden flash of sharp focus. Besides, to imagine, even to *see* live fish is less to visualize a defined object than a movement. "Glide under the green Wave" is one kind of movement; "Graze the Sea weed thir pasture" is another, a fish-eating movement. "Stray," "sporting" — these are two more movements which cause us, kinesthetically, to imagine fish. But the most impressive example of movement (in the sense of Renaissance physics that rest is a kind of positive motion, that of resisting motion) is the "attend / Moist nutriment." It is the absolute of un-motion — gaping, pompous, and wonderfully ridiculous in the calm, successful confidence of the expectation, in the animate immobility. To imagine a shellfish is not to imagine seeing it, but to imagine being it.

Milton tends to see things in motion, or in arrested motion, with more of the painter's passionate craft of depth and breadth of relationship than the camera's art of focus. In the rich combination of the practical and the magical in the building of Pandemonium, we are forced to see, even while the fabric rises, incidental external details (like the golden roof that recalls the barbaric Temple of Neptune in Plato's *Critias*), and the negative comparisons from future history — until suddenly, even while the structure still rises, it stops (like some elevators): "Th' ascending pile / Stood fixt her stately highth." Or consider the arrested motion of the great parade in hell:

> Mov'd on in silence to soft Pipes that charm'd
> Thir painful steps o're the burnt soyle. (I, 561f)

It is the illusion of the total experience which Milton aims at, and not through any intensive visualizing of immediate surface details which could then represent the whole experience. He must see things in their depth and breadth of shadow and line. And he certainly sees things through hearing and touching, through responding imaginatively to the eloquent movements of things, as they are, and as they are in the background and foreground of history. Above all, he visualizes through hearing — through the "voluntary," deliberate discipline and the free grace of improvisation that together move thought and action in a harmony of words:

> Then feed on thoughts, that voluntarie move
> Harmonious numbers.   (III, 37f)

> if all be mine,
> Not Hers who brings it nightly to my Ear.   (IX, 46f)

The great importance attached to visual imagery owes much, and rightly, to the traditional view that sight is the chief of the senses, most closely allied to reason, and further elevated by the traditional relationship of eye to soul and light to God. Plato and Aristotle both agree on this, and confirm for Western civilization the view they inherit. But both make significant qualifications that the student of poetry will do well to ponder. In the *Timaeus* Plato gives sight its traditional precedence by associating it with knowledge of the physical universe, "whence we have derived all philosophy." But then he goes on to relate the physical universe to the moral universe in terms of harmony. By observing the circuits of intelligence in the heavens, he says,

by learning to know them and acquiring the power to compute them rightly according to nature, we might reproduce the perfectly unerring revolutions of the god and reduce to settled order the wandering motions in ourselves.   (47 C)

And then he goes on to amplify this point when he speaks of sound and hearing, which are "appointed to this same intent." Speech contributes "in the largest measure," but music, including poetry:

for the sake of harmony . . . whose motions are akin to the revolutions of the soul within us, has been given by the Muses to him whose commerce with them is guided by intelligence, not for the sake of irrational pleasure (which is now thought to be its utility), but as an ally against the inward discord that has come into the revolutions of the soul, to bring it into order and consonance with itself. Rhythm also was a succour bestowed upon us by the same hands to the same intent, because in the most part of us our condition is lacking in measure and poor in grace. (47 CDE)

Aristotle in the *De Sensu et Sensibili* has the same attitude toward sight as in the *De Anima*. It is the superior sense — but then he qualifies, and in a basic way, though it is nevertheless peripheral to his main approach. Sight is superior in "direct effects" and for supplying the wants of life:

but for developing intelligence, and in its direct consequences, hearing takes the precedence. . . . For rational discourse is a cause of instruction in virtue of its being audible, which it is, not directly but indirectly; since it is composed of words, and each word is a thought-symbol. (437 a)

This is not merely a difference between traditions of oral and written pedagogy, but involves the basic nature of language, which must be a system of sound-symbols for the ear before it can be a system of sight-symbols for the eye; and the prior system, we sometimes perhaps need reminding, can never be entirely supplanted by the sight-symbols. Aristotle does not say this last, but he notes that those blind from birth may still be capable of considerable intelligence, but not those born deaf and dumb.[13]

In poetry, it seems certain, we see truly only through hearing, which draws in all the other senses. Imagery may perhaps be thought of as a kind of human dialect of the soul in the body, and rhythm as the pilot of the meaning which causes the whole body to participate.

Milton writes with the conscious impersonality of a great artist performing under the auspices of Muse the demanding and elevating tasks of a great theme. He does not dwell in a finical way on any single poetic moment, but no moment is lost in the pattern of the whole. Milton's relations with his Muse must be accepted as a literal fact that is also a rich and finally inscrutable fact. He is not making empty ceremonial gestures of polite antiquarianism — though he may seem to be doing so both to those who split his poem into conscious and unconscious meanings, and to those who are inclined to speak of Milton's consciousness as if he were a carpenter following a blueprint which can be *exactly* recovered by research into the poem and his life. The true eloquence Milton aspires to requires getting beyond self, and this is as necessary to the poet for an imaginative return to the true sources of nature and self as to the great figures in this drama.

But the poet does not forget the state of his world, as it now is, and works through conflict, and the impurity of the negative, and the impurity of false eloquence and mixed eloquence — with the pressure of relationship and history upon every phrase. And still, if the imaginative return is possible and real, as to Milton it certainly is, it cannot be achieved naturally, as an unindebted act of intelligence and will. There is the Muse, and the composition is at night, and (though we do not learn the fact from him) in the dying and dead times of the year: in the natural darkness of season and person, which requires and receives irradiation in order to see the invisible. (I speculate, not too seriously, that the darkness of the true poet bears some humble analogy with the apparent darkness of God's "unapproached" light.)

But whatever his private and public rituals, and whatever his attitude toward these, Milton does construct a poem of extraordinary complexity that is at last most impressive for its clarity. I have labored at the complexity and I do not apologize, for not to have done so would have meant for me becoming conscious of a limited clarity. I have not been satisfied with the descriptions of Milton's style that emphasize its simplicity and urge vigilant surrender on the reader. (In these matters history alone will not save us, for there is not a critic alive who can read as if the eighteenth, the nineteenth, and half of the twentieth centuries did not exist.) One does not have to practice surrender to Milton, he commands it; one has to practice vigilance.

To slight his complexity is to slight his precision, and it is the very exacting exactness of his complexity that creates the true clarity. It is a profound clarity which no age or man can master and exhaust. It is a clarity which never fails to carry *through* the complexity (and in this he radically differs from Donne), a clarity which is always the sure master, perhaps one might even say the source, of the complexity. This does not deprive his subtleties of their value, of their contributions in depth and breadth; a clear, known form is, like meter, a guide, but not an answer that can be substituted for process. Milton has a secure metaphysical grasp of the principle, the center, which can admit all kinds of surface complexity, and indeed must, to prove his grasp; he justifies the great theme *in* the process of mastering idea and texture in the perspectives of the whole cumulative weight of the epic structure, and in the traditions of human understanding which give life to and draw life from their embodiment.

Milton's mastery of perspective is intellectual but it must, and does, express itself physically in the poem. We have already examined some cases of perspective controlled in the management of scene and character, in the relating of local context to larger context, in the management of texture and the management of structure, in the imagery, in the diction that achieves transparency through the masterpiece of decorum uniting immediate and total answerability. Examples could be multiplied and observations, I have no doubt, both extended and refined. But I intend only one further extension; it has been implied in much of the preceding treatment. Milton's imagination maintains a distinctive control of the perspective of distance and of space. In detail it is physical, remarkably so; in concept it is intellectual, with space, it seems to me, an aspect of time. He presents the immediacy of the moment in the conscious perspective of time.

Things are held at an epic distance; if they approach close they are nevertheless always seen in the perspective of that distance, in the dimension of God's announced Idea of time. By allusion, epic simile, the constant outward thrust of the imagery, by countless structural references — the events in the foreground which are the immediate dramatic medium are related to eternity. It is a poetic demonstration of the concept of time in the *Timaeus* — "a moving likeness of eternity." It is helpful by way of distinction to refer to a striking moment in one of Milton's early poems,

"At a Solemn Musick": "That undisturbed song of pure concent."
It is an example of beautiful style "presented," "projected" — and
believably possible from another context by a skillful master of
words. This is not demonstrable in any way I know, and so I
must merely assert that other poetic statements in Milton are different though as polished and as formal; they have less of the
personal and they are less possible as the projection of a detachable moment. Part of the distinction, I imagine, is in the built-up
quality that proves itself as a sustained thing, not needing to ex-
ploit the moment for effect, yet always appropriate to the moment in its place in the whole continuum. (I think of the cellist
who has mastered a fine tone and can manage some extraordinary
moments, but cannot manage and modulate the tone so that its
mastered qualities will endure through a strenuous composition.)

In *Paradise Lost* there are many detachable moments that are
projected with striking beauty. Time seems to stop, and the illusion grants the enclosed moment a great intensity, which is always
modified significantly as the moment re-enters the continuum of
time. An obvious example is the sudden illusion of magnification
in Satan's encounters with Death and with Gabriel. Some more
important examples, which occur most liberally in hell, are the
beautiful military review of the fallen angels marching forward
in the momentary unification of music and discipline, with the
illusion of past and present and future boldly but despairingly
fused into one; or the whole building of Pandemonium, and the
sub-moment of Mulciber's fall; or the whole experience of Paradise as a beautiful but impossible moment in time, with sub-
moments complete in their purity, and others, like Eve's dream
or Adam's praise to Raphael of Eve's apparent absoluteness; or
the creation by Sin and Death of the causeway between hell and
earth; or the sustained moments of many of the epic similes
which rise out of the narrative to furnish great adventures in
perspective. All of these, and countless more, gain enormous intensity from being seen both as they immediately are and as they
are in the unfolding perspectives which lead finally to God's Idea
of time, which includes as a smaller circle man's creation, fall,

and redemption. The great circle, which begins with the creation of the angels, and proceeds from God to God, is described as finally ending thus with the last judgment:

> Hell, her numbers full,
> Thenceforth shall be for ever shut. Mean while
> The World shall burn, and from her ashes spring
> New Heav'n and Earth, wherein the just shall dwell
> And after all thir tribulations long
> See golden days, fruitful of golden deeds,
> With Joy and Love triumphing, and fair Truth.
> Then thou thy regal Scepter shalt lay by,
> For regal Scepter then no more shall need,
> God shall be All in All. (III, 332ff)

Under this positive vision of the whole, the powerful play of Satan's immediacy is contained while given the full expression that dramatically demonstrates its opportunism, its essentially negative evil. He has no real place to go, as his syllogism of despair argues; he vacillates between an impossible stasis and a real retreat. The great assertions of individual will which, with their counterplay of conscious and unconscious inner conflict, endow him with the illusion of dramatic being, drive him inevitably to allegorical being. He is drawn gradually into the mechanical existence of his unwilled creations, Sin and Death. It is part of their structural role to show this, for their allegorical being constitutes a kind of stable measure; but their author changes, to become more like his images. When they first meet at the gate of hell Satan ungallantly declares that he has never seen "Sight more detestable then him and thee." But when he returns to find his success anticipated by their "connatural" sympathy, he expresses unreserved admiration for their work, for their very selves, and for their relationship to him:

> Fair Daughter, and thou Son and Grandchild both,
> High proof ye now have giv'n to be the Race
> of *Satan*. (X, 384ff)

He has been demonstrating the logic of sin, the thraldom of self, the progressive deaths of spirit and will; now he passes on to the final mechanistic demonstration, his role in the mass meta-morphosis. At this point he equals the abstract grotesqueness of Sin and Death, and he is himself a monster illustrating an allegory. The infernal trinity do more than parody the supernal trinity and true creation (though I agree with Mr. Tillyard's recent obser-vation that they do this); they demonstrate another order of being, the crude mechanistic existence of allegorical being. Their career constitutes a negative proof that also has some bearing on Milton's attitude toward the imagination; for they oppose, in a mechanical metaphor cut off from true reality, the whole imagi-native vision of true creation and the true poem, with its degrees of metaphor leading up to the great source which allows imagi-native freedom, under love and order, to the human and natural.

The moments not detachable from time are less gorgeous and exciting, freed from the dramatic burden of intensity. I think of the Son's volunteering for sacrifice, of the contrasting forward march to music by the loyal angels in heaven, of the reconcilia-tion between Adam and Eve, of Adam's final recital of his lesson:

> with good
> Still overcoming evil, and by small
> Accomplishing great things, by things deemd weak
> Subverting worldly strong, and worldly wise
> By simply meek; that suffering for Truths sake
> Is fortitude to highest victorie,
> And to the faithful Death the Gate of Life.   (XII, 565ff)

The whole of Book VII is the great example. The Creation oc-curs as an authentic miracle which can take itself for granted. Everything is easy and natural and right. All the creatures do the typical things, which are interesting for themselves, but are loved because they express the order and harmony of the created world. There is no extravagance of image or diction or rhythm. By con-trast the building of Pandemonium is a dazzling piece of self-conscious conjuring.

But there are two other moments that are perhaps more sig-nificant in their contrast. First, the intoxicated extravagance of

image and diction that celebrates the infernal creation by Sin
and Death; especially this:

> The aggregated Soyle
> Death with his Mace petrific, cold and dry,
> As with a Trident smote, and fix't as firm
> As *Delos* floating once; the rest his look
> Bound with *Gorgonian* rigor not to move,
> And with *Asphaltic* slime.   (X, 293ff)

And then, the beautiful and quiet moment of natural description
presented by the simile which concludes the consultation in Pandemonium:

> Thus they thir doubtful consultations dark
> Ended rejoycing in thir matchless Chief:
> As when from mountain tops the dusky clouds
> Ascending, while the North wind sleeps, o'respread
> Heav'ns chearful face, the lowring Element
> Scowls ore the dark'nd lantskip Snow, or showre;
> If chance the radiant Sun with farewell sweet
> Extend his ev'ning beam, the fields revive,
> The birds thir notes renew, and bleating herds
> Attest thir joy, that hill and valley rings.   (II, 486ff)

The natural beauty is as innocent here as in Book VII, but
packed down into this moment is the human consciousness of
change, of the certainty of uncertainty. The intense moment that
prolongs day is made intense by the knowledge that it is a moment;
man responds joyously as a part of nature because he is in the
moment, but it is a mixed joy because he knows about time. And
so the reader shares fallen feelings with these angels; he participates in the experience, which is his experience too, but he is also
outside it by virtue of the controlled perspective and its comment
on this illusion. He will marvel at Milton's imaginative sympathy,
but he will remember other moments: and he may remember particularly the delayed morning of the night-foundered skiff, the
long summer's day, which ends, of Mulciber's fall; and the image
that concludes Mammon's speech, the true and false illusion of the
echoes in the craggy bay after the tempest; and he may be re-

minded later by the images of false light; and by Satan's sea finding a shore in the dubious light on the border of chaos, and by evening and morning in Paradise; and by the unknown beauty of the fruit of Paradise described in an image drawn from the known beauty on the edge of the border of change:

> On which the Sun more glad impress'd his beams
> Then in fair Evening Cloud, or humid Bow,
> When God hath showred the earth.   (IV, 150ff)

And by the final sunset image that formally begins human time and the long day's dying.

The wealth and variety of the answerable style is a vision of the whole, a vision that can accommodate natural beauty, and the necessary discipline in heaven and on earth, and the extravagant hope for man (who is made *to delight*, "and delight to Reason joyn'd") — it is an affirmation of hope in God's love for creation, and a sober realization of the now under the great promise of Time. The *poetic* authority for the great vision of time is also poetic authority for the answerable style. This may be seen in its most direct expression in the passage that follows the Son's free offer to die for man:

> His words here ended, but his meek aspect
> Silent yet spake, and breath'd immortal love
> To mortal men, above which only shon
> Filial obedience.   (III, 266ff)

The variety is unity through the sanction of the immortal love for the mortal under obedience [14]: with the stage, the focus of the feelings, successfully human, allowing the full play of human interest in the drama of freedom, fall, and redemption under the sanctioned perspective of love fulfilling justice. It is a vision that demands love from the style, under an Idea that authorizes and encourages love for created things, and does not require love for the Idea to dry up all other love. It holds to a Platonic insistence on the responsibility of reason, but with no drawing back from the natural and material; man knows God because God has given man the true means, which have dignity.

In his style Milton can trust the springs of the natural, because the "simple" end loves the sensuous and passionate means to it, and does not withdraw its love completely from the means that tend away. Beauty is not blotted out of evil: the fallen angels lie like autumnal leaves "that strow the Brooks / In *Vallombrosa*"; and Mulciber's fall is neither an "unconscious" beauty nor merely (as I have thought) a deliberate irony — there is a place for that beauty finally. Love is the solution of the insoluble. The vision that can contain the necessity and beauty of Eve, the certain but not necessary fall, through misdirected love, and the certain but not necessary redemption in love, can contain in true perspective the individual beauty of each created part in the harmony of the whole creation. Song and dance in heaven express the same harmonious relationship between part and whole:

> No voice exempt, no voice but well could joine
> Melodious part, such concord is in Heav'n.   (III, 370f)

>   mazes intricate,
> Eccentric, intervolv'd, yet regular
> Then most, when most irregular they seem.   (V, 622ff)

When Adam becomes conscious that he has been created, he feels with a knowledge as spontaneous as love that he is happier than he knows, and at the end of the poem he knows that he is happier than he knows. The last two books are not to be explained away historically, as the esthetic result of the seventeenth century's being more interested in biblical history than is the twentieth century. These books fulfill the rhythm of the poem, and they satisfy two kinds of time; they allow Adam a necessary interval to convalesce as man and hero under the aspects of human history and eternity. During this time he becomes a conscious tragic hero (both actor and spectator) accepting, with all passion spent, fully man's condition, and he himself now a fully experienced man; and becomes a mythic hero reborn; and finally becomes man, with all his history behind and before him.

The complex is the dramatic, the dust and heat of the world trying truth in no simple contest. But the clarity shines through the complexity. The style returns through full complexity to a source beyond innocence, without losing any of the wisdom of the whole experience — or the knowledge that it must be lived through again and again.

NOTES

Notes for "The Garden"

[1] Paul Elmer More, "The Theme of 'Paradise Lost'," *Shelburne Essays,* Fourth Series, p. 243.
[2] *Milton,* pp. 282, 284.
[3] As in the *Timaeus,* 77C: "Now when the higher powers had planted all these kinds as sustenance for our nature, weaker than their own, they made throughout the body itself a system of conduits, cut like runnels in a garden, so that it might be, as it were, watered by an incoming stream."
[4] *The Garden of Cyrus,* Chapter IV; Everyman edition, pp. 218-20.

Notes for "The Fall"

[1] *Christian Doctrine,* Chapter VIII.
[2] *Tetrachordon;* in the Columbia *Milton,* IV, 159.
[3] The capital letter is of course not significant here.
[4] Columbia *Milton,* IV, 90, 92-93.
[5] *Ibid.,* IV, 76.
[6] *On the Making of Man;* in *Nicene and Post Nicene Fathers,* Second Series, V, 411-12, 407-8.
[7] *The Creation of the World,* LIII.
[8] *Christian Doctrine,* Chapter VII.
[9] Columbia *Milton,* IV, 74.
[10] *Ibid.,* IV, 98.
[11] *Ibid.,* IV, 100.
[12] *Ibid.,* IV, 93.
[13] *Either/Or,* translated by Walter Lowrie (Princeton, 1944), II, 179-80.
[14] *City of God,* 14, 5.
[15] *Summa Theologica,* I-II, Q. 77, Art. 4.
[16] G. R. S. Mead, *Thrice Greatest Hermes* (London, 1949 reprint), II, 12.

Notes for "Answerable Style"

[1] Or as Aristotle says: "Actual knowledge is identical with its object: potential knowledge in the individual is in time prior to actual knowledge

but in the universe it has no priority even in time; for all things that come into being arise from what actually is." (*De Anima*, 431a.) Or: "Now 'prior' and 'better known' are ambiguous terms, for there is a difference between what is prior and better known in the order of being and what is prior and better known to man. I mean that objects nearer to sense are prior and better known to man; objects without qualification prior and better known are those further from sense. Now the most universal causes are furthest from sense and particular causes are nearest to sense, and they are thus exactly opposed to one another." (*Analytica Posteriora*, 71b–72a.)

[2] This is conveniently reprinted in *Milton Criticism*, ed. James Thorpe (Rinehart, 1950), p. 321.

[3] *The Achievement of T. S. Eliot*, Second edition (1947), p. 90.

[4] *Kenyon Review*, XI (1949), 387.

[5] Thorpe, p. 320.

[6] *Ibid.*, p. 331.

[7] *Timber*, "The Dignity of Speech."

[8] *Religio Medici*, Everyman edition, p. 18.

[9] "The Dignity of Speech."

[10] Thorpe, p. 323.

[11] "Mr. Eliot and Milton," *Sewanee Review*, LVII (1949), 9.

[12] "The Music of Milton," *Philological Quarterly*, XXVI (1947), 342.

[13] And he says at the beginning of *De Interpretatione* (16a): "Spoken words are the symbols of mental experience and written words are the symbols of spoken words."

[14] As I think back I see, what is encouraging, that this was essentially the point I was making in my comment on Milton's hymn to light, though at the time I thought I was making a limited observation. I said then, "in Milton's lines the impersonal and universal strain toward the individual and personal, but within the freedom of discipline and measure, which assert the universal."

INDEX

165